The Teen Spirit Guide to Working with Mediumship

Ceryn Rowntree

SOUL
Rocks

Winchester, UK
Washington, USA

First published by Soul Rocks Books, 2015
Soul Rocks Books is an imprint of John Hunt Publishing Ltd., Laurel House, Station Approach,
Alresford, Hants, SO24 9JH, UK
office1@jhpbooks.net
www.johnhuntpublishing.com
www.soulrocks-books.com

For distributor details and how to order please visit the 'Ordering' section on our website.

ISBN: 978 1 78279 414 1
Library of Congress Control Number: 2014945524

A CIP catalogue record for this book is available from the British Library.

Design: Lee Nash

Printed and bound by CPI Group (UK) Ltd, Croydon, CR0 4YY

We operate a distinctive and ethical publishing philosophy in all
areas of our business, from our global network of authors to
production and worldwide distribution.

CONTENTS

*For my amazing family and friends, and especially for my mum, dad,
Jamie, Shadow, Kali and Shelley*

Introduction

One of my mum's favourite stories about me is the one where we were walking along the beach one night. I pointed up at some lights over our heads and shouted: "Janey, look at the lights, aren't they pretty?!"

The problem was that no one else could see Janey, and most of the people passing by thought I was completely crazy!

I had imaginary friends for as long as I can remember, but to me they weren't imaginary at all. I could see them as clear as day and talked to them all the time. As I got older, they became less clear but I always knew there was someone with me, and there were some nights I would wake up terrified because I knew someone was in my room but had no idea who they were or how to find out.

I always knew that there were people, or Spirits, with me but for a long time I struggled to understand what they were doing there, how to talk to them and how to listen to those people who were hanging about in the corner of my room that no one else knew about.

Maybe you've picked up this book because you have stories like mine; or maybe you're interested in talking to the Spirit world but don't know where to start. I believe that people of all ages come into contact with Spirit Guides, helpers and loved ones from the Other Side regularly, and although not everyone will recognise those helpers and want to get to know them, some of us just can't ignore them!

I've always loved reading about the Spirit world but found that all of the books out there are aimed solely at adults and made working with Spirit sound either terrifying or like really hard work when I was younger. This book is very different to that. It will be honest and sometimes that will mean talking about experiences that weren't much fun, but hopefully that will show why it's so important to look after yourself when working with Spirit.

I was lucky growing up because most of my family was interested in spiritualism and some were even mediums themselves. But all through my teenage years, when I was most desperate to understand more about the spiritual part of myself and start developing my connection to the Spirit world, people told me to wait until I was older. Even when I went along to a spiritualist church to find out more I was told to come back with an adult, or when I was sixteen.

Some of my friends were interested in spiritual things but when a group of us tried meditating I was the only one to see or experience anything. Some of my friends thought I was making it up and the rest looked at me as though I was a freak!

It was as though the Spirit world was there, trying to talk to me but just out of my reach, and I couldn't do anything about that because no one else thought I was old enough! But then everything I read about Spirit Guides and Angels made me think that they know better than we do, so surely if they were trying to talk to me then they must have thought that I was ready?!

Eventually I developed my connection with the Spirit world in a way that was right for me. But if my experiences have shown me anything it's that there's nowhere near enough help out there for young mediums.

I really believe that anyone can communicate with their Guides, Angels and other spiritual helpers no matter what their age, location, hair colour or favourite sandwich! But it's important to do that safely. Dealing with the Spirit world can be difficult and scary, but it doesn't have to be as long as you do it safely and in a way that is right for you.

I hope that this book will help you to better understand the Spirit world and your own connection to it, and to find the best possible way for you to work with Spirit. It can be a scary journey at times but I promise it can be a lot of fun too, and one that will almost definitely help you to feel better about yourself in the long run.

Thank you to everyone who has played their part in bringing this to life, especially to Alice Grist who helped make my biggest dream a reality and to Laura Payne, the very first reader of this book!

With love, light and blessings,

Ceryn

www.cerynrowntree.com

Chapter One

Death

It might not be the cheeriest place to start but in a lot of ways, death is where the Spirit world begins. For a lot of people death is what first makes them interested in working with and hearing from Spirit and, to put it bluntly, a lot of being a medium is all about talking to dead people.

The death of a family member, friend, or pet often makes people think more about their own lives and what will happen to them when they die. And the more we think about that, the more we begin to wonder whether those people we have lost are still around, and are still with us.

There are a lot of different ideas about what happens when someone dies, and where they go after that. If you look at things in a very black and white way then all we can say for certain is that death means one day someone is living and breathing as normal, and then suddenly they're not. When someone dies, part of them disappears and all that is left behind is their physical body, no longer breathing or moving. Some people believe that's where life ends, but I know that's not the case. And if you're reading this book the chances are that you have a sneaking suspicion about that too.

Someone I worked with when I first started to develop as a medium used to talk about death as being a change and not an end, and I've always thought that was a good way to describe it.

For those of us who believe in the Spirit world, death is the thing that takes us out of this world and into the next. Our physical bodies are amazing things, but they aren't built to last forever, and for that reason we can only live here for a certain amount of time.

But that doesn't mean that once our physical bodies die

everything about us dies. Our physical bodies can walk about every day, eat breakfast, talk out loud, and do hundreds of thousands of other amazing things. But it's not just whether you have brown eyes, perfect teeth or one leg shorter than the other that makes you who you are; it is a different part inside of you – your soul or Spirit.

Your Spirit is made of energy so doesn't live in just one part of your body but throughout your whole self. It is responsible for a lot of what makes you you, and since that Spirit isn't physical it doesn't 'die' like your body but continues to exist, just in a way that those of us still living can't always see or hear quite so easily.

Think of your body like a balloon: if that balloon went down you wouldn't be able to throw it around or see it anymore, but the air that had been inside wouldn't disappear; it would just exist in a different way to how you had been used to seeing it.

What happens when we die?

We all know what happens to our bodies when we die, but what happens to the rest of ourselves is a bit of a mystery. And although I've experienced and been told some of that, I don't suppose I'll know exactly what happens until I head off to the Spirit world myself.

When we die, our Spirit moves out of its physical body like a ball of pure energy which can move much more quickly and easily than it could have before. A lot of people who have witnessed someone dying say they've heard a whooshing sound, seen a light or mist, or have had a very strong feeling that the person was standing next to them; more than likely what they've experienced is the person's soul leaving their physical body and heading out to the Spirit world.

There's a TV movie about the medium James van Praagh that I've always thought describes death really well. It shows a man lying in a hospital bed surrounded by his family; a few seconds in, the monitors around his bed start to beep and the people in

2

the room begin to cry and hug one another. But as they do that a dog runs down the corridor and jumps up onto the bed, where the man sits up within his body and says hello, fussing him and stroking the dog. Then he stands up, looks at the family around his bed and leaves his body behind to follow the dog out into the corridor. Outside is a big crowd of people in all sorts of old-fashioned clothes who are all excited to see him, hugging him and shaking his hand. He starts to talk to them and then walks away down the corridor with them (including the dog!) towards a big bright light.

And the people who greet us from Spirit aren't necessarily people we've known here; often older relatives who passed away long before we were born are among the people coming to meet us, and remind us that they love us and have been watching over us from the Other Side.

I don't suppose we'll ever know exactly what happens when we die until our own time comes, but everything I've ever seen or heard of makes me think it's a lot like that movie scene. And I hope so...because as sad as I'll be to leave people behind, I do love the idea of all of the friends, family members and pets that I've lost waiting for me when my time comes.

Losing someone close to you

Losing a friend or family member is one of the worst things in life. It can feel as though there's a huge hole left behind and, at least to start with, can seem as though that hole will never get any smaller, and you will never feel any better.

When someone we're close to passes away, it can be hard to remember the happy times without feeling sad or angry that the person is no longer around, and it's often difficult to see how life can ever be the same without such an important person.

I wish I could say that working with the Spirit world makes that sadness go away, and stops us grieving when we lose someone, but unfortunately that's not true. I work with Spirit every day but it still hurts to know that I won't be able to hug some of the people I care about, or that I won't be able to see them or hear them in the same way I used to.

Sometimes I do get little signs to show that my loved ones in the Spirit world are around and looking after me, and sometimes I even get full messages from them helping me out or trying to make me feel better if I'm going through a tough time. But although signs and messages like that *always* brighten my day, it's not the same as having a cuddle from my nanna, or talking to my granddad about all of the things I always meant to ask him.

Even the best medium in the world will tell you that our loved ones in the Spirit world don't talk to us 24/7, maybe because they know that we have lots of other things to do with our time – and because they do too – but also because they understand that grieving, and learning to live with loss, is one of the biggest lessons we will ever learn.

Unfortunately, there are no rules on how long it takes our loved ones to come back and say hello from the Other Side, and that can be very hard when often we just want to know that the person we've lost is OK or is still with us. Some Spirits come straight back, passing messages on or leaving little signs that they're still around, but some can take months or even years to come back and say hello. That can be very difficult for the people left behind, and makes many people wonder whether there really is such a thing as life after death.

If someone you love takes a while to let you know they're OK, it's not because there's anything wrong with them or because they don't want to talk to you. Sometimes when people reach the Spirit world they have a lot of work to do, or need to take some time out to heal and recover from whatever caused them to pass over to Spirit. And sometimes the people we love know us better than we know ourselves, and recognise that coming to say hello too soon would be too painful or upsetting for us.

Grief is one of the worst feelings in the world and of course we

4

never ever forget the loved ones we have lost, or get over wanting to see and spend time with them. But over time the pain of losing someone does get better and we become stronger. And for that reason, grief is an important thing to go through. Because if you can go through the worst pain in the world, and stay standing, then you can do absolutely anything you put your mind to.

For me, the death of someone I love is still heartbreaking. But it does help to know that the people I love haven't gone very far and are still about looking after me. Not only that, but I'm certain that the time will come when I see those people again, so it's not really goodbye but more of a see you later and those are always a little bit easier to deal with.

Why I know this for certain

It's all very well for me to tell you that your loved ones are still with you, thinking about you and trying to tell you they love you from the Spirit world. But if you're anything like me, you'll want to know how I know that for certain.

The first death in my family that really, really affected me was my nanna's; my family is very close so losing my amazing nanna when I was eighteen was very painful for everyone. And although I know that I was very lucky to keep her for so long, it didn't make the first birthday without her 8 AM *Happy birthday to you* phone call or the first Sunday without her baking any easier.

About nine months after my nanna died I had the most amazing dream about her; I remember walking into her kitchen and seeing her by the stove. In the dream I started crying and she gave me a big hug and asked why I was upset; she was right there so there was no need to be sad. She then sat me down at the table so we could have a good chat and a catch up. That was lovely, but what made this dream amazing was that it was so real; I couldn't just see my nanna, or hear her voice, I could smell her perfume and her hairspray, feel the wool of her cardigan, the papery softness of her skin and her just-permed hair in ways that I thought I had completely forgotten. I woke up convinced that it hadn't just been a dream, but an actual meeting with my nanna.

But that isn't the only time she's talked to me while I was sleeping; a few years later I was going through a tough time when I had another vivid dream about my nanna. In the dream she told me everything would be OK but I just carried on complaining. Eventually, she drew a symbol in front of us and told me that it meant patience and faith, and that those were my lessons in this lifetime so that's why I just had to sit back and wait, but believe her when she said that everything would be OK. When I woke up I could picture the symbol she'd shown me, but since I've never been the best artist had no way of getting it down on paper. So instead I went to the computer and typed "patience, faith, Japanese" into Google images. Imagine how surprised I was when the exact same symbol popped up on the screen!

And my nanna isn't the only one who has proved that she's still with me. A few years ago a friend of mine passed over suddenly and unexpectedly. Although he hadn't been one of my best friends, he was a good mate who I'd spent some good times with over the years, and we were all devastated to say goodbye to him. At the office where I worked, a book of remembrance was set up and one night; before I headed off to the spiritualist church I went to every week, I wrote a message in the book. A few hours later a medium at church came to me with a young man who'd passed over suddenly and very recently, and described my friend perfectly...then told me almost word for word what I'd written in the book.

That same friend was a huge fan of the band Elbow, and we both loved their song "One Day like This". Since he died, almost without fail, that song comes on the radio or TV whenever I'm feeling low or in need of a hug, or whenever I'm about to do something really important.

6

I could go on and on and on with these stories, and happily would! But although it's nice to hear about the experiences that have convinced other people about life after death, the only thing you can ever truly believe in is the proof you get for yourself. When you have your own experience that makes you think "yes, that's the person I lost definitely coming back to tell me that they're OK and that they're still with me," that's when you will well and truly be able to believe in the Spirit world.

Chapter Two

The Spirit world

We've talked a lot about Spirits and the Spirit world, but it's difficult to really understand the idea of life after death without having an idea what life on the Other Side is like. It's another of those things that none of us will ever really know until we get there ourselves but the messages I've had, as well as what I've read, heard, and seen myself in dreams or meditations have given me an idea of the basics.

The Spirit world has lots of different names; the Other Side, Home, Heaven, but all of those (and any others you hear along the way) mean the same thing; they talk about the place where our Spirits come from and where they go back to after our physical bodies die.

Every creature on Earth (and probably even creatures on other planets too, but that's another story!) is a Spirit. While we are living on Earth, that Spirit lives inside our physical body so it can experience human life and learn lessons that wouldn't be possible anywhere else.

Imagine your body like a car that takes you on the journey through life. You need that car to visit all the places and do all the things that the driver inside (your Spirit) has planned for your journey but the driver gets to experience that journey and decide where the car should go and when.

But while your physical body can be easily seen and touched, your Spirit is different. It is made up of energy and just like the light that comes from a bulb or the heat that comes from an oven, that energy can't always be seen, heard or felt on its own. In the same way our bodies must have food, air and water to work properly, our Spirits need other things instead, like love and positivity.

Sometimes when we're sleeping or meditating, or if someone is particularly ill, the Spirit takes a journey away from its physical body for what is sometimes called an out of body experience. This doesn't happen to everyone, and usually happens when someone is unconscious because for a person to act and think normally, their Spirit needs to be inside of their body.

When a Spirit moves about on its own it can travel anywhere it wants to as fast as it wants. Think about the teleportation you see in sci-fi movies, or apparition in Harry Potter – in the Spirit world you need only think of where you want to be and there you are!

There is a saying that our loved ones in Spirit are only ever a thought away. That is partly because in the Spirit world we can go anywhere we want with only a thought but also because just like Spirits, thoughts are energy. And although we can't always see or hear them, in the Spirit world thoughts are no different from the things you say out loud and your Guides, helpers and loved ones are always listening out for your thoughts and keeping an eye on you in case you need them.

That doesn't mean they watch or listen to everything you do or say though... I don't know about you but my thoughts are pretty boring most of the time, and I really don't think my Guides want to see me on the toilet, or first thing in the morning! But just like a good friend who's always there when you call or a text, your Spirit friends are only a thought away if you need to ask them for help.

Just like our souls, the Spirit world is pure energy, so it doesn't have the same rules about time and space that we have here. Not only can we go wherever we want just by thinking it, but because our souls never die, we don't have to worry about rushing around to get things done by a certain time.

That's not to say that we sit around doing nothing all day...imagine how bored we would get if we did that forever!

We all have jobs to do in the Spirit world, although they're very different from jobs here. Everyone works because they want to and because they enjoy their jobs rather than because they have to, and all Spirit jobs are done to help others, or to help make the Spirit world an even more beautiful and wonderful place.

Another big difference is that there is no money in the Spirit world, which can take a little bit of time to get our heads around for those of us here on Earth who spend quite a lot of time thinking and worrying about money! In the Spirit world, though, we can create anything we want just by thinking about it so don't need money. We can do or enjoy whatever we want to just by thinking about it and often, when we stop trying to impress other people or be part of the in crowd, we start to realise that we don't really need that much after all.

When someone we love passes away, leaving their friends and family members behind, it's easy to worry that they will be alone on the Other Side. But our friends and family in Spirit aren't just the people and animals we know from this life but also the ones we've met in our previous lives, so we have more friends and family there than we would ever have time to keep up with in the physical world!

Animals are an important part of the Spirit world too and, just like people, the Spirit world is home to all the animals that have ever lived or will ever live. So, along with all of the cats, dogs, goldfish, rabbits, cows, sheep, elephants and tigers you would expect to see, there are extinct animals like dodos and dinosaurs, and others like dragons and unicorns that we have only ever heard about in stories and legends. And since there is no anger or aggression in the Spirit world, and no need for anyone to eat, all of these animals – including people – live quite peacefully alongside one another. I love the idea of that and, although I don't want to go to the Spirit world for a long time yet, it's something I'm really excited to see.

Almost everyone who visits or says hello from the Spirit

world talks about what a wonderful place it is, not just because it's so beautiful but because everyone there is so nice and everything is so lovely. That might sound too good to be true, but when we move to the Spirit world we let go of our fears, anger, pain and worries, and without any of that it's much easier for everyone to be much happier and kinder.

But the Spirit world isn't just made up of people and animals, there are many different types of beings there, and it's important to understand the differences between them before you start working with Spirit.

Spirits

Many of the energies you will come in contact with from the Other Side are just like you and me, but without physical bodies. They are the people who have passed over to the Spirit world, or who have never lived a physical life but have Spirits just like ours. And remember, you are just as likely to come across dogs, cats and other animals from the Spirit world as you are people.

These Spirits often look and sound very similar to the people and animals you meet every day. Without physical bodies, there's nothing to keep Spirits looking a particular way, so it's really up to them how they decide to look. However, most people choose a very similar appearance to the one they had here, mainly because they're comfortable that way and because it's how their loved ones will recognise them. Imagine if I got over to the Spirit world and decided I wanted to look like a supermodel; that would be great until I tried to get a message to my family, who might be a bit confused by a tall blonde woman saying she was me!

Children who pass into Spirit grow up just as they would have here but can also choose their appearance when they come back to visit. Sometimes they choose to give messages looking the same as they did in life, but sometimes they appear as they would have been if they had continued to grow up in the physical world.

Spirits can also appear in whatever clothes they want to and feel most comfortable in, which sometimes means talking to people who appear in very strange or old-fashioned clothes. However, some like to come back in clothes we will recognise, such as an outfit they're wearing in a photograph we have; my great great granddad moved from England to America in the early 1900s and somewhere in my grandma's house is a photograph of him dressed like a cowboy. I'm pretty sure he didn't always dress that way but it's the most memorable photo of him I've seen, and so on the odd occasion he has come to talk to me, he's dressed as a cowboy!

The main difference between the way our loved ones look in Spirit and how we remember them is that any pains or illnesses related to our bodies vanish as soon as we pass into the Spirit world so Spirits never show any signs of old age, injuries or illnesses. Sometimes a Spirit will talk about an illness or injury but that's just to help prove to whoever they're talking to that they are who they say they are.

One of the strangest things about talking with the Spirit world is that the people and animals who talk to you aren't always the ones you expect to hear from; often they aren't even Spirits you know! But it's important to remember that our families on the Other Side are much bigger than in the physical world and, because they don't have to worry about time or space in the same way we do, it's easier for them to look out for our families for much longer than we could.

I first started going to spiritualist churches a couple of years after my nanna died, but would get very few messages from her. Most of the messages I got came from my great granddad, who was very close to my dad but died before I was born. Sometimes that seems strange – why would someone you don't know or only ever met once or twice, like your grandma's old next door neighbor, want to come and talk to you? But really it's lovely to think that there are so many people on the Other Side who care about you, even though you may not remember them. Over the years since he first started talking to me, I feel as though I've got to know my great granddad and I love the fact that he cares about me just as much as anyone else in my family.

You might have heard about Spirit Guides, and that's something we'll talk about later. But it's important to remember that your Guides and helpers are often normal Spirits just like your friends and loved ones from the Other Side. The only difference is that Guides have a special job to do in working closely with you to help and guide you through this lifetime.

Angels

Although Angels are made up of pure energy like Spirits, they are also very different. While Spirits are a lot like the people or animals that they were when they lived here in the physical world, Angels are made up of pure love and light and exist solely to help, heal, protect or guide us.

We often imagine Angels to look just like people, but with wings on their backs, halos or rings of light over their heads and a beautiful bright light all around them. In reality, some Angels are much more comfortable appearing as flashes or balls of light, or in another way that we recognise as being an Angel.

All Angels have beautiful energies, and the best way I've found to tell that there is an Angel with me rather than any other type of Spirit is that everything feels easier when they are around; my worries or aches and pains disappear, I feel safe and I have a much better idea what to do with things I might have been worrying about before. But the best way I can describe the feeling of an Angel being near is that it feels just like having the biggest, safest and most loving hug you can ever remember... beautiful!

Just as we have Spirit Guides, each of us has a Guardian Angel whose job is to look after you, keep you safe and help you through life. You might have heard stories about people who have been in very dangerous situations and have heard a voice telling them to react a certain way, or have felt themselves being pulled or carried away by someone they couldn't see. The voice or the rescuer they talk about is usually their Guardian Angel.

Nature Spirits

We've all read stories about faeries, elves and other creatures of nature and, if you were anything like me when you were small, you wished you could have your own Tinkerbell to make friends with. But what makes you think that those energies aren't real?

Nature Spirits come in lots of shapes and sizes, from elementals (like faeries and pixies) to plant and tree Spirits. And just like everyone else in the Spirit world they can choose how they appear to us, so while some people will see them just as cartoons tell us we should, others will see balls of energy, flashes of light, something completely different.

Nature Spirits protect the natural world and help us keep the natural balance of things so they will often work with us in a very different way to other Spirits, helping to heal us and guiding us to work more closely with nature.

Ghosts

A lot of people think that all Spirits are ghosts, but that's not always true. All souls from the Other Side can leave us little signs or do things to let us know they're around us, but 'ghosts' are slightly different.

The Spirits that we usually call 'ghosts' are the ones that stay with a certain place or object; not only do they tend to make things move about, but they can often be seen or heard for themselves in those places too. The difference between those Spirits and our loved ones and Guides who pop over from the Other Side whenever we need them just to say hello or to help us, is that 'ghosts' are Spirits who are stuck on Earth for some reason.

Usually Spirits get stuck because they choose not to pass over to the Other Side. Maybe they have spent their whole life being frightened of death or think they've done something awful on Earth so are frightened of what they might find, or maybe they feel as though they have some unfinished business they need to sort out before they can pass to the Other Side. Instead, they choose to stay here but can't live fully in the physical world without a body so are just stuck almost between the two worlds, which must be very frustrating and explains why some 'ghosts' can be quite angry or miserable or do so much to attract attention to themselves – making noises and moving or breaking things. It must be hard to be somewhere that you used to belong but not be able to do any of the things you used to, recognise anyone there or have anyone recognise you.

It's important to remember that some stuck Spirits can be quite angry or even dangerous, so if you choose to work somewhere that you believe to be haunted it's especially important to protect yourself and your energies, particularly once you've started to open up to other parts of the Spirit world.

Chapter Three

Mediumship

A lot of people think that being a medium means sitting in a dark room asking if there's anyone there. In real life though, mediumship is usually much less scary than that! It's often easier to explain what a medium isn't, so I'll start there.

Firstly, being a medium doesn't mean being able to tell the future; it would be amazing to be able to look into a crystal ball and see exactly what the future has in store, but life isn't usually that easy!

No matter what people may say, mediums don't know everything. Talking to the Spirit world puts you in touch with a lot of wisdom and information we wouldn't otherwise know, but they don't tell us everything, and sometimes they don't even tell us what we want to know, at least not until it's the right time to do that.

Being a medium also doesn't mean being psychic, or able to read someone else's mind. Sometimes you can tell what someone is feeling by the energy they give out, but that isn't really anything to do with the Spirit world. At other times the Spirit world will tell us how someone we're dealing with is feeling, but that doesn't make you psychic.

And lastly, being a medium doesn't mean getting an easy ride through life. We all come here with lessons to learn and although Spirits are always there to help and guide us, being a medium doesn't mean that you get all of the answers. If it did I would've asked for the winning lottery numbers a long time ago!

But if it doesn't tell you everything you need to know and doesn't let you see into the future then why would you want to be a medium? I know I'm biased, but I think it's a great thing to be.

For starters you can help people, by showing them that they're not alone, and that the people they love are still very much with them and looking out for them, no matter what may have happened. Bringing that hope and happiness to someone is a real privilege and I don't think anything I've ever done has given me so much of a buzz as giving a lady a message that her grandson was fine now and that all of the signs she was getting were from him.

And it's not just about what you can give to other people, there are some selfish parts too. I once heard a medium called Gordon Smith say that whenever people asked why he was so happy, he would tell them it was because he knows that death is nothing to be frightened of. And if you're not frightened of death, then what is there to be scared of? I agree with him, but I also think it's more than that. Everyone goes through bad patches and sad times, but once you know that there are so many people out there looking after you, and trying to help, it's hard to feel scared or sad for too long.

For a long time I didn't believe I was a medium, because I didn't *see* Spirits in the same way I did my friends and family who were still here. It didn't help that a lot of the mediums I spoke to would talk about seeing or hearing Spirits all over the place.

It took me a while to realise that just because I get messages from Spirit in a different way doesn't mean I'm not a medium. Every medium picks things up from Spirit in different ways and none of them are any better or worse than any others.

The psychic senses

A lot of people talk about using the psychic senses to pick up information from Spirit. There are six psychic senses and for most people one or more of these senses is naturally stronger than the others, although the others can grow stronger as you work with them more and more.

The word 'clair' is French for 'clear', so the psychic senses are really called clear seeing, hearing, feeling, knowing, smelling or tasting.

Clairvoyance
Clear seeing is about being able to see the Spirit world, or the information that they give you. For some people that means physically seeing Spirits as 'ghosts', shadows or what I like to think of as the sparkles at the corners of your eyes; for others it might mean seeing images within what is called your mind's eye.

It's different for everyone, but when I physically see Spirit faces and figures, they look very different to people on the street; I see them more as outlines, almost as though they're drawn in the air in front of me in light.

You might see them differently though, or maybe you don't see faces or figures at all. I know a brilliant medium who only ever saw the Spirit world as balls of light for a long time. He learned a lot about each Spirit by the colour and size of the orb, and picked up messages by looking at the orbs and asking them to move in different ways depending on what they had to say.

Of course some people do see fully formed people, animals, Angels and other figures. When I first started developing as a medium I was desperate to see Spirits but the idea of someone jumping out to say hello when I was at home on my own terrified me, especially since I thought that those people would turn up looking the way they had when they passed away (*The Sixth Sense* has a lot to answer for!). In my experience so far, and the experience of every other medium I've spoken to though, that's not the case.

If you could make yourself appear anyway you wanted, would you want to look old, ill or scary? If it were me I think I'd want to look my best! Maybe that would mean looking younger and healthier, or maybe looking the way my loved ones would best recognise me.

However you see the Spirit world, the chances are that you

will start seeing them in the same way many people do; out of the corners of your eyes. I often catch a glimpse of something but when I turn my head to look properly, it's as though there is nothing there. Sometimes those things look like shadows or sparkles or even just wavy, like a haze on a hot day.

It can be very frustrating to catch things out of the corner of your eye but it's important to be patient, and to focus on trying not to look too hard. Over time the Spirit world will draw closer so that you can see them easier and more clearly, but usually only as long as they know you're not frightened to see them.

People who teach mediumship often talk about seeing into the Spirit world through our 'third eye', which is in the middle of our foreheads. That can mean that when we're trying to develop our clairvoyance, we get a bit of a tickle or prickle in that spot. As long as it doesn't cause you any problems, or last too long, that's nothing to worry about, it's often just your third eye waking up.

Clairaudience
Clear hearing is about being able to hear the Spirit world and like clairvoyance, there are different ways to do that.

If you're someone who hears Spirits out loud you may hear someone calling your name or music being played. In my experience that's one of the ways Spirits first try to catch your attention, even if they wouldn't usually talk to you clairaudiently. After all, shouting someone's name is an easy way for us to get their attention so why wouldn't the Spirit world do the same?

Clairsentience
Clairsentience means *clear sensing* and can be even wider than either of the previous two spiritual senses because there are so many different ways to feel and again, you're just as likely to get an impression of feeling something through your mind as you are to actually feel it.

Even when I tried not to have anything to do with the Spirit world I could often still feel them around. At first I found that freaky and a bit scary, but now I understand it's just proof that Spirits have always been there for me even when I didn't want to recognise it.

I first felt the Spirit world physically; I would feel someone brush past me, put their hand on my shoulder or stroke my hair. Usually that would feel exactly the same as if a living person was to do those things, except that there would be no physical person there. Since then I've been told that the person stroking my hair is almost always my nanna, so it's always a lovely feeling when that happens.

Often clairsentience is more about just sensing someone there and using that to pick up information about them. If you've ever had your eyes closed but known that there was someone near you, even though you couldn't hear or see them, then you'll know exactly how that feels.

The third type of clairsentience is actually feeling physical conditions or symptoms. Sometimes Spirits talk to us in that way to help show who they are – if someone suffered a lot with a bad leg their friends or family might recognise a medium mentioning that. At other times the Spirit world will put physical conditions 'on to' us to help pass messages to people who are still in the physical world and may be suffering from those problems, or to explain a particular situation such as having 'butterflies, 'itchy feet' or a 'pain in the neck'.

Clairalience

Clairalience means being able to smell things that have been sent by the Spirit world. The most common thing that people smell is cigarette smoke when no one around is smoking, although it's possible to smell flowers, perfume, food or anything else Spirits send our way.

For a lot of people smells trigger very strong memories, and

Spirits often send smells to us to help bring back those memories. However, smells that are too strong to ignore is another good way for the Spirit world to catch our attention if they don't think we're paying attention.

Clairgustance
Clear tasting is when the Spirit world puts tastes into our mouths, or give us a very strong memory or idea of exactly how something tastes. I know it sounds a bit odd but tastes can mean a lot and again bring back very powerful memories and, for that reason, they're clever ways to get someone's attention, or give a clear message.

Claircognizance
The last spiritual sense is 'clear knowing' which is about knowing information but having no idea how you know it. Even more than with any of the other senses it can be difficult to tell which of these knowings come from Spirit and which are your own gut or intuition…either way though as long as you protect yourself properly these knowings won't steer you wrong.

Everyone is capable of developing all of these senses and even if you've never done any development work as a medium, you'll probably have read one or more of the descriptions above and thought: "But that's happened to me!" Well then, when you start your spiritual development, why not focus on that sense first?

Developing your senses
Developing your psychic senses isn't that different to developing your physical senses, it's just about focusing on them one at a time. Try this exercise to start working on your senses.

1. Close your eyes and take a few deep breaths.
2. Concentrate on your breathing, keeping it slow and steady.

3. As you breathe in and out concentrate on what you can feel around you; what is the temperature like? Is there a breeze around you? Is the air damp or dry? What is underneath you, behind you or to the side of you and how does it feel?

4. Next concentrate on how you feel on the inside? Are you tense or relaxed? Mentally work down your body from the top of your head to the tips of your toes and pay attention to how each part feels.

5. Think back to the last time someone touched your hand. How did it feel? Try to concentrate on that memory as hard as you can and think, how would it feel if someone touched your hand now?

6. Move your attention to tastes, and concentrate for a moment on what you can taste; is the taste of anything you've eaten or drank still in your mouth? If so, concentrate on it and exactly how it tastes and what that taste makes you think of.

7. Whatever you can taste right now, think about your favourite food and how that tastes. Concentrate on every part of that taste, how it feels on your tongue and in your mouth, what the taste makes you think of or remember, how it makes you feel, and just enjoy that taste for a few moments.

8. Now focus on smells; take a few deep breaths and focus on what you can smell right now; what different smells are in the air? What do they make you think of? If there is more than one smell in the air, concentrate on each of the smells around you in turn and give as much attention to each of them as you can.

9. Think about your favourite smell in the world, and imagine that smell as much as you possibly can – how does it make you feel? What does it remind you of? How does it feel in your nose? Concentrate on it for a little while.

10. Next focus on the sounds around you. Start with the sound of your own breath, and anything else you can hear from within yourself. Then listen to the air around you; what can you hear? How does it sound? Is it high or low, fast or slow? How does it make you feel? Concentrate on each of the sounds around you in turn and listen to them as hard as you can.

11. Now concentrate on the sound of your own inner voice. How do your thoughts sound? Whose voice do they speak in? How does that voice make you feel?

12. Quiet the voice for a while and try to focus on the quiet within your mind. How does that sound? How does the quiet make you feel? Sit in that quiet place for a few moments.

13. Now picture the face of your best friend in your mind. Picture their face as clearly as you can and notice all of the details you can.

14. Now open your eyes and look straight ahead of you – what one thing do you see first? What shape is it? What size? What details do you notice about it? Try and notice as much as you can about it until you could close your eyes again and see it perfectly.

15. Finally look around you and notice your surroundings as a whole, focus on the details and on exactly what you can see. If you see colours what do those colours make you think of? What details do you see around you?

This whole exercise can take as much or as little time as you like and can be done in any order you like (as long as your sight is last), or even one sense at a time if you find it easier. Once you're finished though, take a few minutes to bring yourself back to the present moment completely. Wiggle your toes and have a stretch before you try moving very far.

Different ways to use mediumship

No matter which spiritual sense you focus on there are many different types of mediumship and ways that you can practice as a medium once you have developed and have the confidence in your own abilities to do so.

Traditional mediumship

The most traditional type of mediumship involves sitting with one or more people and passing the messages you receive from the Spirit world on to them. Although it's always helpful to try out any other types of mediumship that you're interested in, this is probably the most common and straightforward way to connect with Spirit so it's worth giving it a go if you really want to use your skills to help other people.

Spiritual healing

One common way to connect with the Spirit world is to bring healing energy through from them into yourself, another person, animal or thing. There are lots of different forms of spiritual healing with many different names, but all of them do the same thing; draw positive energy from the Spirit world and use it to heal. However, it's important to remember that spiritual healing is no substitute for a qualified doctor so should never be relied upon to diagnose someone or make them better.

Paranormal research mediums

Many mediums are drawn to help people who have passed away but aren't ready to move into the Spirit world. Those mediums will usually work with paranormal research or ghost-hunting groups who explore places that seem to be haunted and explore the reasons for the haunting to try and soothe whoever or whatever is causing problems and help them move over to the Spirit world.

Channelling

Some experienced mediums open themselves up to become channels for Spirit, meaning that they allow Spirits to talk through them. This can be a dangerous thing to do, and for that reason I'd only recommend channelling for experienced and confident mediums who are comfortable protecting themselves fully.

Physical mediumship

Lastly, some mediums will develop physical mediumship, when they allow Spirits not only to speak through them but also to take over their face so that anyone looking at the medium would see the Spirit person instead. Again, letting a Spirit do this can be dangerous so it's best left to experienced mediums and only tried in the company of someone even more experienced that you feel completely safe with.

Chapter Four

People

Anyone can communicate with the Spirit world. I always think that being a medium is lots like singing; some people are naturally better at it than others but with a bit of training everyone can do it. Sometimes though, it can be easier to have to do that training than to be a naturally gifted medium.

If you're drawn to becoming a medium the chances are that you're naturally quite in tune with the Spirit world, but that doesn't mean you won't have to work at it. No matter how good we are at something, practice can always make us better. Later in the book we'll talk about the best places to go for training, and about how you can test and develop yourself as a medium.

But just because everyone can communicate with the Spirit world it doesn't mean that they do, or even want to. Although opening up to the Spirit world is becoming more and more common, a lot of people are still scared, don't believe or are just plain not interested. And although those who aren't interested generally won't bother you too much, people who are scared or openly don't believe in the Spirit world can cause both developing mediums and experienced ones a few problems. In fact, often the living bother us mediums far more than anyone on the Other Side!

No matter how much proof you have that the Spirit world is definitely there and using you to communicate, there will still be people who don't believe. For the most part that's pretty sensible of them; after all, if I told you the sky was green would you believe me? I'm guessing the answer is not until you'd gone outside and checked for yourself! A lot of people won't believe in the Spirit world until they've had their own proof, and that's absolutely fine. But remember that your job as a medium isn't necessarily to convince everyone you come across that the Spirit world exists, so sometimes the only thing you can do with someone who talks about how much they don't believe is to smile, shrug and go help someone else instead!

You will get some people who won't think that's good enough; there are people out there who not only don't believe in the Spirit world but will go to any lengths to try and convince other people to believe the same...including sometimes mocking or being mean to you. To put it bluntly, it is *never OK* for someone to make you feel bad, regardless of whether they are talking about your beliefs, your skin colour, your sexuality or the size of your bum! But although it doesn't make it any easier to deal with, it's important to remember that the people who tend to be the meanest and the loudest are generally the most scared of everyone.

I've come across plenty of those people, and I've tried any number of different ways to deal with them. So to try and save you going through some of the same battles that I did, here's how those different tactics worked out for me:

- Getting angry back generally helps no one; if anything it makes that person the winner. More than likely they're just trying to get a rise out of you, and by losing your temper you're giving them exactly what they want. Besides, if you're anything like me, getting angry or losing your temper with someone will only make you feel better for a few minutes before you start to feel bad and just a little bit silly for getting so worked up.

- Cockily telling them that you know best and threatening to prove it almost never works out well. No medium can promise to produce a particular message from a particular Spirit and it's more than likely that a loud non-believer would need very very specific proof before they changed their mind. If you can't give them exactly what they're looking for? Well that's just proof that you've been lying all along as far as they're concerned! But even if you did tell them exactly what their Great Auntie Mabel had on the left-hand corner of her mantelpiece, some people would still refuse to believe you and would only go away telling people that you'd snuck into their auntie's house before she died...it's probably just not worth the hassle!

• There's always the option to just walk away. I'd love to say that I'm always mature and sensible enough to do that because it is often the best way to deal with it, especially if the person is really winding you up to the point of no return. But I'm far too keen on having the last word to be able to do that every time. And of course it's not always possible to walk away from these people or situations. If you are more sensible than me though, and it feels like the sensible thing to do then there's no shame in smiling, shrugging your shoulders and walking away to see or talk to someone who is more deserving of your time and energy!

• In my experience the absolute best way to deal with someone who is completely arguing against your beliefs, even if they are being a bit rude or mean with it, is to treat them with the same respect that you would like from them. I have a very good friend who completely and utterly disagrees with my beliefs and with what I do; a few years ago we reached a point where every time we were together we would find ourselves debating with one another and going round and round in circles. Eventually we realised that we would never agree but that all of this debating was really tiring, and a waste of the time we spent together. Now when his trips to church, or my work as a medium, come up in conversation we just listen, respect that it's an important part of someone that is important to us, and then move on to talk about something else.

Unfortunately, not everyone who disagrees with your

beliefs will be as easy to deal with as my friend, but the principal of respecting their beliefs in the way you would like them to do for you is the same. Taking a few deep breaths to calm your temper or your emotions and then saying something along the lines of "Well, that's your opinion and I respect that, but I think we'll have to agree to disagree on this one" before changing the subject can be a tough thing to do, but it's often the best way to react. If they know they won't get a rise out of you they're more likely to leave you alone and to respect your opinion a bit more.

While some people will mask their fear with mickey taking, name-calling and nastiness, others will be all-out terrified to hear that there are dead people out there who can see and communicate with us, never mind that you would choose to talk to those people! That can be really difficult to take, especially if the people who react that way are the ones you care about. It's important to reassure them that just because you talk to the Spirit world doesn't mean that you do that all of the time and that you would never want to do or say anything that would scare them. Maybe you could explain to them that although there are scary stories out there and some people do have negative experiences, you do a lot of work on protection to make sure that you – and they – are kept safe from anything dangerous, and offer to show them some protective tips if they ever do feel scared. Otherwise though it's often sensible just to respect that, in the same way you have friends that you don't talk to about certain bands or TV shows, maybe your work with the Spirit world just isn't something to talk to that person about.

Who knows, one day the people who are most scared of your work with Spirit may become interested or lose that fear. If and when they start to ask questions it's best to ease them in gently – steer clear of any stories that might be considered scary to start with and focus instead on the nice healing stories that you have, like a certain song coming on the radio at exactly the right time, the smell of your grandma's favourite flower appearing in your house on her birthday or the message you gave someone to let them know that their very ill friend was now safe and healthy on the Other Side. Do what you can to make it as non-scary as possible for them but be honest, and be prepared for a lot of questions – as you probably already know, once someone becomes interested in the Spirit world there's a lot they want to know!

The opposite end of the scale is those people who hear that you work with Spirit and just won't leave you alone! Some people will act as though being a medium makes you the coolest person in the world and means that you have all of the answers, while others seem to think that making friends with a medium means that they have their own personal hotline to the Other Side and to anything they might want to know. Hmm…

It's always nice to be liked and it's easy to let people like that tag along because they make you feel popular, especially if you're someone who has had to put up with being called a freak in the past. But remember that true friends will like you and want to spend time with you because of who you are, not what you can do and how you can help them. I've made some amazing friends, including my very best friend, through my interests in Spirit and I'm certain that you will meet some amazing people too, but the people who ask you for free card readings every time you see them, or who only ever want to talk about their problems and what their grandma in Spirit has to say about them just might not be friends with you for the right reasons.

It's up to you what you do about that of course, and if you're happy to occasionally feel as though someone is taking advantage of you then that's completely your business. One thing that I've learned about people like this is that they are often quite draining and can really start to affect your energy after a while. If you want to keep them in your life then that's absolutely up to you but my advice would be to keep them at arm's length and not rely too much on them as you would your real friends.

All of that said, in my experience most people are very interested to meet a medium, will ask a couple of questions and then fire away and tell you all about the time someone they knew saw a ghost, or the absolute proof someone they knew got that their grandma was still with them long after she'd passed into the Spirit world. And that's great – I've heard some of the best and loveliest stories during conversations that started that way, and have also made some great friends through conversations like that with people who were genuinely interested in Spirit.

The best advice I can give when it comes to integrating physical people into your interests and work with the Spirit world though is, just like anything, choose the people in your life that you talk to about it. You probably already know the people who are interested in similar things, and those who would love you and support you whatever you did with your time, so they are probably a good place to start!

If anyone does say anything mean or ridiculous about your beliefs then remember that they aren't talking about you but about their own beliefs, and more often than not they are speaking from a place of fear. Try not to take their comments too personally and remember, everyone is entitled to their own opinion...even if it's wrong!

The most important person of all

When it comes to developing your connection with the Spirit world though, the most important person you will ever deal with is yourself. Being a medium can be tough sometimes, and it can be scary too, and it's important not only to protect yourself (more on that shortly) but also to get to know, understand and respect yourself too.

For starters, it's always a good idea to think about your own beliefs and where they came from. What was it that you heard, saw or experienced to first make you think that maybe there was such a thing as life after death? And what is it that convinced you that was definitely true.

If you haven't had any proof of your own yet and are starting to feel more mad than medium, then why not ask for some? Ask Spirits to give you a particular sign that they're with you, or to put something in your mind that you should look out for as being a sign from them. Remember that the Spirit world is always keen to help you and unless you're absolutely certain in yourself that the Spirit world exists then how can you ever really trust your connection with it?

When thinking about your own beliefs don't just think about life after death but about the other things people will undoubtedly link in to the Spirit world once you start talking to them: Angels, ghosts, past lives and anything else in that field that takes your fancy. If you're interested and want to know more then by all means do some research. But if you don't want to read up on any or all of them, that's fine too; knowing about past lives isn't a must for working with Spirit, and if something is really important then you'll be encouraged to learn about it from the right source when the time is right.

Your beliefs and ideas about Spirit and all the subjects connected to it will undoubtedly change and develop as your journey continues, so just because something seems right now doesn't mean that won't change over time.

If you're still looking for your own proof it's important to ask for the signs you would like from Spirit. The Spirit world don't always perform on command and sometimes they like to give you their own signs which you'll become used to, but there's no harm in asking for particular signs from particular people or helpers to show you that they're with you.

Think about a particular smell or song you associate with someone; specific words or memories you would like a loved one to bring as proof if they come to talk to you through another medium, or of anything else that reminds you of a particular someone. Try to make your signs quite specific and as special to you as you possibly can, and don't feel silly or bad about asking either out loud or in your head for Spirit to bring those things to you. Then sit back and wait for the Spirit world to communicate with you. Remember there's no such thing as coincidence, and if you ask your granddad to bring you a particular type of flower to let you know he's with you but don't tell anyone else what you've just asked, then you walk outside to find that flower randomly sitting on your doorstep, it's more than likely your granddad saying hello.

Think also about what particular things mean to you. If you decide to develop your connection with Spirit far enough to pass messages from the Spirit world to loved ones on this side, you'll often find they start to follow similar patterns and include similar signs or symbols. And although there will be times that the messages you receive for other people are specific to them, often those common things come to you time and time again to symbolise the same message.

For example, some mediums get a lot of messages with flowers, and although sometimes those flowers will come through because they were a person's favourite, or have a special meaning to the person receiving the message, often they are an easy way of passing on some particular message such as the time of year of a person's birthday or the anniversary of their death.

I get a lot of animals – and although the animals can belong to the person I'm talking to, or to a house they used to visit, for me animals also represent particular qualities or situations that the person might have or need in their life. For example, a horse can mean support or strength, or a dog can mean unconditional love. When you pick up messages like that it can be difficult to figure out whether it means your meaning or someone else's, so the easiest way is to ask them. I'll often say something like: "I have a big brown horse here. For me, horses often come through to give strength and support for a situation you're going through. If this is a horse that you know though, or if it has another meaning to you, then please take whatever feels right for you."

It's important to remember that common signs are different for different mediums. Probably the best example I can give is colours; to me the colouur blue means protection because it links with Archangel Michael, while purple is healing or wisdom. But I've known mediums who've given me those colours as the opposite, so it's important to trust your own instinct and guidance when it comes to interpreting signs rather than listening to anyone else.

Your own signs

Think about what different signs mean to you. If you're not sure then ask for guidance and see what feelings, people or ideas come through most strongly. Here are some ideas to get you started.

- Colours
- Flowers or plants
- Places
- Animals

Also think about your own signs, how you know that certain people are with you, and what you want to receive from Spirit to know that everything will be OK. Again, if you're not sure then ask and wait for those ideas and signs to be sent your way.

An important part of communicating with Spirits is trust, not just in them and what they have to tell you but in yourself too. Whether you call it your gut, your intuition, your higher self or guidance from the Spirit world, getting in touch with that very clever voice inside you is important for anyone who wants to work and communicate with Spirit, and it's something I would recommend anyone doing before they start to develop as a medium.

That voice (I'll call it your intuition for now) is the one that always says the most sensible and lovely things to you, stops you doing anything silly and lets you know that things will be OK on the days that everything seems to be falling apart. It represents the inner you, the part of yourself that is pure Spirit and is completely free of any negativity or fear. And because of that it is the wisest and most knowledgeable part of yourself; it's well worth listening to!

One of the most important things to remember when working with Spirit is to keep yourself safe, and your intuition is an important part of that.

Your intuition

Take some time to get in touch with your own intuition – first by recognising the voice of your intuition as opposed to your ego or the voice of your fear. During really stressful times, your intuition is the one that says: "Calm down, it will be OK. Just take a deep breath and then we'll work through this," while your fear will run through all of the worst what ifs, tell you all of the ways things could go wrong and generally leave you feeling worse than you did to begin with!

Once you've sorted out which voice is which, take a day or two to listen to your intuition – you might not always be able to follow what it says exactly but at the very least listen to what it is telling you, act on the guidance that feels right and see how much easier life seems when you do that.

And the more you pay attention to your intuition, the more you will be able to hear it, and the easier it will be to be true to yourself and follow that guidance. So give it a go for a couple of days and see how you get on.

Chapter Five

Protection

If you're looking to communicate or work with the Spirit world the single most important thing is to keep yourself safe.

It's easy to forget about something as boring as protection when you're excited about getting in touch with the Other Side; and it's easy to think that you don't need to protect yourself because after all, how can a Spirit person hurt you when they don't have a physical body to punch or kick you and they don't have any germs to pass on to you? Believe me, there are plenty of very good reasons that protection should be the first thing on your to-do list every single day once you start working with Spirit.

What are we protecting ourselves from?

As we see whenever we turn on the news, there are some awful people in the world. And although the majority of people out there are lovely, it's those not-so-lovely people we have to watch out for. Because of them we shouldn't walk around after dark by ourselves, lock our doors at night, and don't leave our phones or iPods lying around in public. And unfortunately, just as there are negative people in the physical world, there are negative energies in the Spirit world, and it's them that we need to protect ourselves from whenever we open ourselves up to Spirit.

The negative energies I've heard of and come across fall into two different groups; one is the people who have crossed over to the Spirit world but are still hanging on to some of the more human emotions of anger or fear, while the second group is made up of Spirits who come from a different and much darker place to the one we would normally work with.

The first group can be difficult to work with in the same way that very angry or unhappy people in the physical world can be difficult to spend time with; they can drain your energy and leave you feeling tired or miserable. However, sometimes part of what's making those Spirits unhappy is their need to talk to a loved one who is still living and apologise to them or give them a particular message. If you are that loved one, or if you're able to help pass on the message then it's a great feeling and often, as soon as the message is passed on you can feel the Spirit's energy lift and they become much nicer to be around.

Sometimes though those messages can't be passed on for one reason or another and the Spirit will hold on to that negative energy. If you find yourself dealing with someone like this all you can do is ask your Guides to take them away from you and help them.

The second group of negative energies come from a darker side of the Spirit world. That isn't somewhere I've ever wanted to go or learn too much about, but I understand is that it's not a nice place and is filled with those energies who have chosen to turn away from all types of love and focus instead on not-so-nice emotions.

The Spirits who come from there tend to have one mission, which is to spread fear and negativity and you can usually tell when one of these negative energies is around because they leave you feeling uneasy to the point of being terrified. However, they also like to play tricks and often pretend to be nicer Spirits so that they can sneak their way in to work with you before showing their true colours. To me, the fact that they might trick me into trusting them only to then hurt me or cause problems is the scariest thing of all about these energies. But again, as long as you protect yourself each and every time you start to work or communicate with the Spirit world then you shouldn't need to worry too much about those negative energies.

Going back to those not-so-nice people we mentioned earlier, would you ever throw your front door open and stick a sign at the end of the street saying "open house, anyone welcome"? Of course not! Well working with the Spirit world without protection would be very similar so please please please don't ever do it!

Intention

The most basic way to protect yourself and your energies is to make sure that any time you go into communicating with the Spirit world you do so with the best possible intention, in other words that you're doing it for the right reasons.

Say for example you were trying to get in touch with Spirit so you could scare someone, or to prove just how damned good you are. Neither of those are positive reasons for making that communication...and although you might attract some very nice energies, you're also likely to attract the kind of arrogant or scary Spirits that will be thinking similar things. However, if you are communicating with Spirit so that you can help people who are sad or unhappy in some way, or to help prove that there's no reason to be afraid of death, you are much more likely to attract positive energies who want to do equally good things.

There's a very popular ghost-hunting TV programme which I stopped watching a long time ago (although to be honest it was far too scary for me anyway!) because I hated the way they spoke to Spirit. The presenter would shout: "If there's someone there hit one of us! Come on, if you think you're so big and clever, push us or hit us."

I'm not one to judge, but that seems kind of stupid to me...would you ever stand in the middle of the street and shout something like that? No. Why? Because some bigger, scarier people than you might hear and do just that! And it's exactly the same with the Spirit world. Of course they were trying to scare people and prove that there were ghosts in the room with them. But in the same way that any normal person would avoid someone shouting that in the street, all that shouting really did was scare away the more positive energies, clearing the path for the other ones to step forward and take advantage!

Think about why you want to work with the Spirit world. Is it because you want to help people? Maybe it's because you've lost someone yourself and would like to know for certain that they haven't gone too far and are still around you? Or maybe you're just plain curious and want to know more? All of those, and many others, are perfectly good reasons!

If, however, you want to be a medium just to show how cool you are, to earn lots of money or become world famous, to get one up on someone or to scare people then it might be an idea to stop now. I'm not saying that those reasons mean you should never ever try to communicate with Spirit, just that it would be an idea to take a break and really think about why those things are so important to you, and whether being a medium, or anything else that brought you those things, would ever make you truly happy.

How to protect yourself

There are many ways to protect yourself, some of which are below:

Archangel Michael

One of my favourite ways to protect myself is to call in Archangel Michael, the Angel responsible for protection, strength and safety. Some people will tell you there are very specific rituals and prayers that you have to use when calling on Michael, but in reality it doesn't matter what words you use or whether you call to him out loud or in your head, as long as you ask Archangel Michael to bring you his protection, and then visualise him doing just that.

If you Google Archangel Michael you'll see all sorts of different images of him, because people often see individual Archangels in the way that makes them most comfortable.

However, most people agree that Michael is big, blond and carries a shield and sword. So once you've asked for his protection, visualise a big, blond man with a sword and shield standing with you, looking out for you and keeping you safe from anything but the most positive energies.

Michael almost always brings a beautiful blue light and energy with him, so if you imagine any of the ideas below as being blue it helps bring in Michael's energy and strengthen them too.

Just like others in the Spirit world, the Archangels have no physical bodies, so can help many people at once. So don't ever think you shouldn't call on Michael because someone else may need him more, he is more than happy to help everyone who asks for his protection.

Cloak

I'm a bit of a Harry Potter geek, and one of my favourite things in those books is Harry's cloak of invisibility. And although there are no cloaks that make you physically disappear (yet!), we can use a cloak to protect ourselves from negative energies in just the same way as Harry does. Again, just close your eyes and imagine wrapping yourself tightly in a cloak that reaches all the way down to your feet, with a big hood to cover your head too. As you're imagining yourself wrapped in the cloak remind yourself that this cloak is incredibly strong and nothing but the most positive energies possible can ever touch you as long as you are inside.

Bubble

Another way to protect yourself is to imagine yourself in the centre of a bubble of light. Don't just see that light but imagine you can feel it around you too, and know that once you're inside nothing and nobody but the most positive of energies can see, hear or contact you.

Crystals
Lots of people like to have a physical something they can ask to help protect them. Really any item can be used for this, but crystals are especially useful because they have such powerful energies. Many types of crystal are well known for their protective properties, and some of the best are amethyst, tiger's eye, clear quartz, hematite and lapis lazuli. However, I believe that you can turn any crystal into a protective stone just by holding it in your hand for a while and asking it (either out loud or in your mind) to protect you from anything but the most positive energies.

If you use a crystal for protection though, make sure that you cleanse it regularly to keep it working as well as it possibly can. There are lots of ways to cleanse a crystal, so many that I could write a whole chapter on just that!! But there is plenty of information available online about that, so I would encourage you to Google 'how to cleanse a crystal' and use the way that feels best, easiest and safest for you.

Prayer
Whoever or whatever you believe in, one of the simplest ways to protect yourself is to ask – again either out loud or in your head – that energy for protection from anything but the most positive and loving energies.

Your own protection
Take some time to think about what makes you feel safe and how you can use that for protection when you are working with Spirit.

Protection is possibly the most important part of working with Spirit, but it is also a very personal thing and it's important to find what feels best, and safest, for you.

When to protect yourself

It's important to protect yourself each and every time you open up to work with the Spirit World, as well as any time you feel uneasy in any way. But the negative energies we come in contact with in the physical world can be just as draining as negative Spirit energies, so it's a good idea to get into the habit of protecting yourself every day.

Try to get into the habit of running through your protection every morning and again every night before you go to sleep as well as every time you start to work with Spirit.

The more often you protect yourself, the safer you will be and the easier it will become to ask for protection whenever you feel as though you need it. It's almost impossible to protect your energies too much, so asking for protection every day and night just means that you are protected always, and still leaves you free to 'top it up' or ask for extra protection any other time you feel uneasy or uncomfortable too.

Protecting other people and places

Sometimes it's not just ourselves that we want to protect; maybe there are other people around who we can see being affected by negative energies, or maybe there is a particular place that you have to go regularly which doesn't feel very nice.

Protecting other people is just as easy as protecting yourself, and you can use all of the same techniques to protect someone else as you would for your own energies. The important thing to remember is that every individual soul has free will, and that we must always respect that. Sometimes that's very difficult – it's always tough to watch someone you care about make a mistake that you know will hurt them and not be able to stop them, but it's important that we always respect that free will.

There are plenty of ways to send out protection to another person without interfering with anyone's free will. One of my favourites is by asking for protection and then using the phrase "in love and light and for the greater good of all". That's another way of saying that you are asking for this protection for the most positive reason possible but don't want your request to interfere with anything that soul has to learn or experience for themselves.

When it comes to protecting places, one of the easiest ways of doing that, unfortunately, is by keeping them clean and tidy! It may sound silly but the dirtier and messier a place becomes, the easier it is for negative energy to gather like dust. Certain sounds such as bells, singing bowls or even just your own voice singing or chanting positive sounds can be used to cleanse energy. Another popular ways of cleansing a place is to burn the herb sage, which is said to be a very cleansing plant. Sage does burn quickly though, and can leave you feeling a little woozy (not to mention smelling suspicious!) so please be careful if you decide to use it, and please be sure to keep a window open and tell any parents or adults that live with you before you start so they don't think you've been up to no good!

Archangel Michael can also protect a particular place or area, or crystals can help soak up negative energy in a room and change it into something more positive.

Sometimes it can be hard to believe that any of the ideas above will keep you safe. But if you're struggling to have faith in your protection then Archangel Michael is your man! Not only is he able to protect you, but he can also help you to feel stronger and more confident if he's asked. Give it a go and see!

Looking after yourself in other ways

Sometimes it's not just the negative energies in the Spirit world that you need protection from; sometimes things in the physical world can hurt or damage our own energies too, so it's important to keep yourself physically safe, clean and healthy too.

Negativity often affects us more if we're feeling tired, run down or unwell. It's always important to look after yourself but if you're working with Spirit, then it's even more important to ensure that you're eating a good, balanced diet, are getting enough sleep and are doing everything you can to keep your physical body running as well as possible.

And looking after yourself is about keeping yourself safe from negative emotions as much as possible too. All of us will get angry, stressed or upset from time to time, and that's important because it's often those difficult situations and emotions that teach us the biggest lessons. However, it's important to try and minimise those situations and emotions in our lives as much as possible and to spend more time doing the things that make you calm and happy instead.

The most important thing to remember when it comes to taking care of yourself is to trust your own intuition. I'm sure you already know that your intuition will always take care of you and encourage you to do the things that are best for you. It's not always easy to listen to that very sensible little voice, and no doubt there will be plenty of occasions when you can't or don't want to so what it tells you. But following your gut as much as you can is a good way to look after yourself and help keep yourself as safe as possible.

Chapter Six

Opening up and closing down to Spirit

Connecting with Spirit is a bit like finding a radio station; you have to tune yourself into the right frequency before you can pick up what is being said clearly. At first that can be difficult but the more you practice 'opening up' and tuning into Spirit, the easier it will become.

And as important as it is to tune in when you work with Spirit, it's even more important to know how to tune out too. After all, imagine how annoying, or even scary, it would be if you were constantly hearing voices or seeing people around you without being able to shut them out. Aside from anything else, how would you ever get to sleep?

Not only that but tuning into the Spirit world can often make it feel a bit like we're floating outside of our bodies; unless we close ourselves down and tune back into the physical world we can leave ourselves feeling lightheaded and woozy...or worse! A friend of mine once took part in a deep group meditation. At the end the workshop leader didn't tune them back in, just asked them to get up and gather their belongings. Some people found they just couldn't get straight up; while others stood, only to fall flat on their faces because they weren't quite back!

The moral of the story is that not only do you need to take the time to tune in every time you start to work with the Spirit world, you must also take the time to tune back into the physical world every time you stop. And this chapter will give you some ideas about how to do that.

Chakras

Just as we have organs like the heart, lungs and brain to control our physical body, we have energy centres or 'chakras' that control our spiritual or energetic body. Like the physical organs, each chakra has its own job to do and they can only work as well as possible if they are looked after and kept clear and healthy.

The chakras aren't physically visible but each of them has a place in the area around your physical body and blockages or problems with the chakras can lead to physical problems in those areas.

The seven basic chakras are:

- Base or root: This sits just below the base of your spine; to put it bluntly, in the space between your bum and your bits. The root chakra is usually seen as red and is in charge of grounding you and making you feel secure and confident in dealing with the physical world.

- Sacral: The sacral chakra lives a few centimetres below your belly button and is usually seen as orange. This chakra relates to creativity and your ability to connect to inspiration and come up with ideas as well as to all things related to sex.

- Solar plexus: The next chakra up is yellow and sits between the bottom of your ribs and your belly button. This chakra deals with how you feel about yourself, and how powerful and confident you are because of that. The solar plexus chakra is often thought of as the home of your Spirit or 'higher self', which is why we sometimes refer to the most knowledgeable part of ourselves as our gut.

- Heart: This energy centre is green and lives, as you'd expect, in the centre of your chest next to your physical heart. Maybe it's not a surprise but your heart chakra governs love and how connected you feel to other people. When we talk about having a broken heart, that often means that someone or something has hurt us so deeply it has blocked our heart chakra or caused it to close down a little.

- Throat: The throat chakra is located right in the centre of our throat (where your Adam's apple is or would be) and is a blue energy centre. It is responsible for communication and for your ability to speak your truth. If you have something difficult or uncomfortable to say you may find your voice croaking or squeaking, or you may even begin to cough; this is often your throat chakra clearing itself out so that you can speak your truth more comfortably.

- Third eye: Your third eye can be found between your physical eyes, right on the bridge of your nose. It is indigo-coloured and links to intuition and wisdom, as well as to Spirit. It's said that our third eye is the one that sees into the Spirit world so if you are looking to work on your clair-voyance the third eye chakra is an especially important one to work on.
- Crown: Our crown chakras are violet (deeper purple than indigo) and sit right at the top of our heads; the crown chakra is the one that literally opens us up to higher vibra-tions and frequencies as well as being responsible for connecting us to the wider universe.

Everyone sees their chakras slightly differently; some see them as flowers, others as balls, stars or other shapes. Generally, chakras appear as coloured lights which glow and spin at different brightnesses and different speeds depending on how well they are working.

If your energy levels and Spirit are all in tune and working well, those lights will all glow at the same brightness and spin at the same speed, but if one or more of your chakras are out of sync they may be brighter or duller, slower or faster than the others. Sometimes as you 'see' your chakras, they may look a little grubby, or as though they are blocked with something. That's nothing to worry about, it probably just means they need a good cleanse.

But what does all this talk about chakras have to do with

opening up to communicate with Spirit? Because your chakras are responsible for your Spirit and energy levels, opening them up and clearing them out helps you to focus on the non-physical part of yourself and raises your vibrations, helping you to tune in better to the Spirit world.

How to open up

There are many many ways to open up, and just like protection the way that you raise your vibrations and tune in to Spirit will be personal to you. Whatever you decide to do though, the most important thing to remember whenever you open up to work with Spirit is to work on your protection first of all.

From there, you can do whatever helps you feel lighter, brighter and more in tune with Spirit. Some of the ideas that have worked for me or other mediums I know are:

- Imagining a dial inside you and turning that dial up until the general noise and goings on around you start to fade and you tune into a new, much higher 'station' or frequency;
- Imagine taking off some sort of outer layer, like a cloak or a suit of armour. As you make yourself lighter, feel your vibrations rise higher and higher;
- One medium friend of mine would always picture herself stepping out of a bucket of water and up onto a step so she was literally higher up and ready to talk to the Spirit world;
- Ask your Guides, helpers or Angels to come around you and help to communicate with perfect clarity with those who come from the Spirit world. But remember to ask specifically to communicate only with those who come from the light;
- See your crown chakra, the glowing light on top of your head, open out like a flower and see that light shine up into the Spirit world like a beacon welcoming all of those who come from the light to communicate with you.

Remember that as you open up to work with Spirit, you will be relying less on your physical body for a while, although it is still incredibly important! For that reason try not to move about too far at first while you're open, just to keep yourself safe.

Also, don't worry if you don't see or hear anything straight away; allow yourself to open up and then sit quietly for a few minutes and pay attention to anything you see, hear, think, feel or anything else that occurs while you're waiting. You may not get full messages right away but keep track of what you do experience and you'll find that over time these impressions will get stronger and more detailed.

How to close down

It's important to close down your energies every single time you finish working with the Spirit world. Even if it feels like you haven't picked up a lot from Spirit, that doesn't mean that you haven't been open to their energies and don't need to close down and tune yourself back into the physical world again.

Just like opening up, there are many different ways to close down and the best way is the one that works best for you. The simplest way to close down is to do the reverse of whatever you did to open up, but here are some ideas:

- Imagine that radio dial turning back downwards, until the noise and goings on around you become louder and clearer and you tune back into the physical realm;
- See yourself putting on a cloak, suit of armour, coat or another outer layer, and as you do, feel it bring you down to a lower and more physical vibration;
- See yourself stepping into a bucket of cold water, or burying your feet in soil or sand to bring yourself more in line with a physical vibration;
- Ask your Guides, helpers or Angels to close down your energies and bring you back to the physical realm where

those from the Spirit world will be temporarily unable to work or communicate with you until you choose to open up again;

* See a hat or cap being placed over your head to cover the light coming out of your crown and know that with that light blocked off you are bringing your energies back to the physical world and closing yourself down to any communications from Spirit.

However you choose to close down, remember that the most important thing is to surround yourself with protection not only when you open up, but also after you have closed your energy down.

Tuning in your energies

Going through the following meditation will help you raise your vibrations and open up to Spirit then close yourself down again. Sit or lie down somewhere quiet and comfortable where you won't be disturbed for at least fifteen minutes and start by closing your eyes and taking a few deep breaths.

1. As you breathe deeply, ask Archangel Michael to surround you with his beautiful blue light of love and protection, allowing only those who come from the light to step forward and communicate with you. See him surround you with a blue glowing bubble of light.

2. See yourself inside that bubble and feel that beautiful blue glowing light surround and fill you, making your whole body feel lighter and brighter and filled with love.

3. Concentrate on that wonderful light feeling for a few moments and continue to breathe deeply, feeling the light grow brighter and stronger with every breath.

4. As you breathe, see a glowing, spinning ball of red light form below the base of your spine, and know that this is

your root chakra.

5. Focus on that light – how brightly is it glowing? How fast is it spinning? Are there any dark-looking areas inside it? As you concentrate see the beautiful light that fills you mix with that red ball of light cleaning and cleansing it and helping it to spin faster and glow brighter.

6. Once your root chakra is perfectly clean and clear, and is spinning freely and glowing perfectly, move your attention upwards.

7. Just below your belly button is a glowing orange light, your sacral chakra. Focus on that light and again, look at how brightly it is glowing, how fast it is spinning. Are there any dark areas in that ball of light that need to be cleared?

8. Focus on that energy; see the beautiful light of Archangel Michael flow into and through your sacral chakra cleansing it, cleaning it and opening it up.

9. After a few moments notice that ball of orange energy glowing more brightly, spinning more freely as it is now perfectly clean and perfectly clear.

10. Now move your focus up to your yellow solar plexus chakra in the centre of your stomach; see it in the same way you have the others before and notice how clean it is, how brightly it glows and how fast that ball of energy is spinning. Bring Archangel Michael's beautiful energy into your solar plexus and allow it to cleanse, clear, balance and open that beautiful ball of golden energy.

11. Once your solar plexus is perfectly clear, focus upward into the green glowing energy in the centre of your chest, your heart chakra. Take a good look at that beautiful green energy to see how well it is spinning and how brightly it is glowing. Then feel the wonderful energy within you fill that heart chakra and help it to spin more freely and steadily, to glow more brightly and to become

cleaner as any blockages are cleared out and any damage is healed. Continue to focus on your heart chakra until you see it as perfectly clean, perfectly clear, spinning freely and glowing brightly.

12. Now move up to the blue ball of energy that is your throat chakra. See how well it spins and glows, and how clean it is, and then call in the beautiful energy of Archangel Michael to cleanse, clear, open and balance it as it has the other chakras.

13. Once your throat chakra is clean, clear, open and balanced, move up to the glowing ball of violet energy above the bridge of your nose. See your third eye chakra glowing and spinning and then bring in Archangel Michael's beautiful energy to fill it, balance it and open it, while cleansing and cleaning any blockages and healing any issues in that chakra. Fill your third eye chakra with this beautiful energy until it is clean, clear, balanced, open, glowing brightly and spinning freely.

14. Finally, move up to the very top of your head where you will see a glowing ball of indigo light. See that light glowing and spinning, and draw in the beautiful energy of Archangel Michael to flow in and through your crown chakra, opening and balancing it and clearing any blockages. As that chakra opens and clears, see it become brighter and brighter and stronger and stronger.

15. With each of your chakras open, balanced, clean and clear, see those balls of energy grow and grow until they join together in one long strip of beautiful white glowing light which starts below your body, connecting you to the floor, the ground and the very centre of the Earth and flowing through your root chakra right up, through your sacral, solar plexus, heart, throat and third eye chakra up to your crown chakra. As the light reaches your crown chakra see it spilling out of the top of your head,

stretching up to the Spirit world and inviting all those who come from the highest vibrations to step forward and make contact with you.

16. As that light flows through you and around you through each of your chakras, ask your Guides and helpers to step forward and work with you as you try to make contact with those who come from the light.

17. Sit quietly in this light for a little while and see what comes to you.

18. After a while, stop what you are doing and thank Spirit for working so closely with you. As you do so, feel that beautiful white light begin to pull back into your crown and your root chakras, until eventually it is contained completely inside your energetic body.

19. Next, focus on each of the glowing balls of coloured energy within your body and force them to spin a little more slowly and grow a little less bright. Start with the indigo crown chakra on the top of your head, move to your violet third eye chakra between your eyes then down to the blue ball of energy in the centre of your throat. Next, focus on slowing and dimming your green heart chakra, your yellow solar plexus, your orange sacral chakra and your red root chakra.

20. Focus on slowing and dimming each glowing ball of light until you feel their energies slow down and your chakras close down for the time being. Once each of your chakras is moving slower and glowing less brightly, feel your energy levels come back to the physical realm and know that for now you are closed to working with the Spirit world.

21. Even though you are closed down, know that you are still connected to your own Guides, helpers, Angels and loved ones, and to all of the help, wisdom and guidance they wish to bring forward to help you through this life.

22. Before you come fully back to the physical realm, call on Archangel Michael and ask him once again to surround you with his beautiful and perfect blue light of love and protection.

23. Now take a few deep breaths, stretch, wiggle your figures and toes, and slowly bring yourself back into your physical body before opening your eyes when you're ready.

24. Note down any feelings, impressions or images you received while you were open to Spirit.

Grounding

Even after you've closed down to the Spirit world, it may take a while for your energy levels to return to normal and your vibrations to move fully back into the physical. Don't move too quickly and if you feel at all lightheaded, tired or 'floaty', take it easy before trying to move about.

If you're really struggling to put yourself fully back into your physical body the easiest thing you can do is to have some food – even just a biscuit or apple will help ground you – and a glass of water. Another option is to do something really grounded and unspiritual – watch TV, read a magazine or play a game until you're feeling back to normal.

Again, take it easy and take your time, especially when you're first starting. Remember that tuning into and out of the Spirit world can be like exercising; it takes practice and to start with it can be tiring. Make sure there is always someone around (even if it's just in another room) when you first start opening up to Spirit, just in case you find yourself feeling a bit odd in any way.

Chapter Seven

Meditation

Lots of people think that meditating means sitting cross-legged for an hour chanting "ohm" while you listen to peaceful music. If that's something you really want to do and have time for then carry on ohm-ing. But, let's be honest, it may not be the most comfortable way to spend an hour!

Meditation is a pretty big subject which you could write a whole book on if you wanted to, but since it is quite important for getting in touch with Spirit and your own higher self, I will talk a little bit about it in this chapter.

Meditation is about finding a way to quiet and clear your mind and is a really good way of relaxing if you have a lot going on, or of giving yourself some time out if something is worrying you or stressing you out. When it comes to working with Spirit though, meditation helps quiet your own thoughts and worries to allow Spirit to communicate with you more easily.

The most traditional way to meditate is to sit or lie down and breathe deeply, concentrating on your breath until your mind is completely clear. Sometimes that might involve listening to or taking yourself through a guided meditation – sort of a story that helps you feel or imagine yourself in a particular place or situation. Guided meditations can be especially useful if you're looking to meet a certain Spirit, visit somewhere spiritually or get in touch with a particular piece of information. As someone who tends to get quite distracted and find her mind wandering, guided meditations help me to concentrate on just relaxing, although I'm generally pretty rubbish at following written meditations for myself. For that reason I've tried to keep the meditations in this book as short and easy to remember as possible.

As I said before, you can sit cross-legged to meditate, but in my experience that leads to cramp, which isn't exactly relaxing! The best position to meditate in is the one that is most comfortable and easiest for you. For me personally, sitting down doesn't work at all; lying down to meditate sometimes ends with me nodding off but hey, that shows I'm relaxed!

For a long time I really struggled with meditation because I thought that if I wasn't meditating the way the books said I must be doing it wrong. I tried so many times to sit down and meditate but usually either fell asleep or got completely distracted which made me more stressed than I had been to start with and, in turn, made it more difficult for Spirit to talk to me!

I once met someone who told me that she meditated for a whole hour a day...incredibly jealously I asked her how she managed it, and she told me that she started small – ten minutes twice a week up to twenty minutes three times a week and so on until she could happily meditate for an hour a day. Well I tried, I really did. But I even struggled with ten minutes a week! Again that stressed me out, and made me think that maybe I just wasn't cut out for this Spirit-work lark after all.

But then I read a magazine article that changed my whole idea of meditation completely...it said that we don't have be sitting silently, listening to a guided meditation or focusing on our breathing to be meditating. In fact, often one of the best ways to clear your mind and meditate is to do something that you can focus on completely without having to think too much about it. Some good examples are cleaning, exercising, gardening, baking, painting or playing music.

I know it sounds silly but you would be amazed at the amount of very deep, very strong information that comes through to me from Spirit while I'm walking the dog or weeding the garden! The key to meditating while you work is to concentrate on exactly what you're doing, or where you are. This is sometimes called mindfulness, because it is about being mindful of every single part of what you're doing; what you see, what you hear, what you smell, how it feels, why you're doing what you are and anything else that springs to mind.

That may sound like quite a lot to think about, but by the time you focus on why you're washing the dishes, how the water feels, how the cloth feels, what the washing-up liquid smells like, how nice it is to have a clean dish, etc. etc., you'll find that there's very little space left in your mind for other thoughts! I still struggle to be mindful all of the time, but although we're mediums it's important to remember that we're human too, and humans still think. A lot!

Another way I've found to focus my mind is by doing something that I've always loved; daydreaming. Whether it was about winning the lottery, lying on a white beach somewhere, or being swept off my feet by Nick Carter (Google him, he was my number-one crush back in the early '00s!), I've always been good at losing myself in a good daydream. And although daydreams don't relax your mind completely they do switch off the logical, rational part of your brain that worries and thinks too much so stops Spirit from communicating with you clearly. Again, you'd be amazed at how many times my daydreams (although nowadays they tend to be less about Nick Carter!) have been interrupted by messages, communications and full-on lectures from Spirit.

But how do you know when Spirit talks to you through meditation, especially if that meditation involves your mind wandering off on some lovely daydream? The first thing I look for is something that seems to pop up from nowhere, with no logical reason for being there. Other times you will recognise the things that come from Spirit rather than from your own mind because they'll sound different; either you'll hear another voice talking or the words are being said differently to when you usually think. Sometimes you'll just *know* that what you're experiencing is wisdom from Spirit. Often you know that because it feels different, and makes you feel better or more peaceful in some way.

That's not to say that the Spirit world will always say what you want to hear, or that you will always easily be able to tell the difference between what they say and what your own heart or head wants to hear...but the best way to be able to tell the difference between your own thoughts and what the Spirit world tells you is with practice. The more you meditate, the easier it will become to move into that frame of mind, and the more you hear from Spirit, the easier it will be to know when they're talking to you.

So, to start you off with that practice, below are a few short exercises to help you find your own way with meditation.

The first two exercises are more traditional meditations, so find somewhere comfortable where you won't be disturbed for at least fifteen minutes and give them a go. Don't worry too much if you doze off through either of these meditations, or if you struggle to picture anything; the more you meditate the easier it will be to visualise and to fall into the meditation.

Just like any work you do to raise your energy levels remember to take it easy when you first come back from a meditation. Don't get up too quickly and take time to make sure you're feeling back to normal and have grounded yourself before you try to do anything too strenuous.

Basic breathing meditation

1. Close your eyes and begin by taking a deep breath in through your nose;
2. Hold the breath for a moment – just long enough to be comfortable without trying to hold it for too long, and when you're ready take a long slow breath out;
3. As you breathe out concentrate on breathing out any stress, tension, pain or negativity that you are carrying

with you, and instead feel yourself breathing calm, peace and love deep into yourself;

4. Continue to breathe deeply and calmly in and out, concentrating on breathing the negativity out of yourself and breathing positivity in instead;

5. As you breathe listen to the sound of your breathing. Focus on its rhythm and on the peace and calm that rhythm brings to you;

6. Continue to focus on the rhythm and sound of your breath for as long as is possible and as long as feels comfortable. If your mind wanders remember to breathe deeply again, and focus back on the sound and the rhythm of your breathing.

Basic guided or visualisation meditation

1. Close your eyes and take a few deep breaths in and out;

2. As you breathe, imagine yourself on a path in the centre of a forest; it is a beautiful summer's day and the sun filters through the trees. Feel the warmth of the sun on your skin and feel the light breeze as it touches your hair;

3. Look around you and see how beautiful the forest is; notice the beautiful colours of the trees and flowers and hear the sound of birds singing and chattering in the trees above you;

4. Continue to walk through the forest, pausing every now and again to appreciate what a beautiful and peaceful place this is;

5. As you follow the path through the forest you come to a clearing, in the centre of that clearing is a large flat stone;

6. On the stone are a number of items, each of which symbolise something you have been looking for in your life and feel you've been missing. In the centre of the stone is a note with your name on it and you know that

the items on this table have been put here for you;

7. You reach down and pick up a bag that has been left under the table, and into that bag you put each of those items from the top of the table, taking time to look at and touch each item as you do, and understand what that item means to you;

8. Once each of the items are in the bag you put that bag onto your back and turn away from the table, knowing that you carry with you everything that you need for this next part of your journey, not only back through the forest but through life.

9. You walk back through the forest, appreciating how beautiful and peaceful it is and recognising how calm and at peace you feel here. As you walk know that this place will always be here and you can return here anytime you want or need to.

10. Bring your attention back to your breathing and focus on taking long deep breaths. As you breathe feel the air coming into your lungs and feel your chest rise and fall as the air moves into and out of your body.

11. As you concentrate on your physical body, bring your attentions back to your physical body and to the room around you; focus on the temperature, anything you can hear or smell and on how your body feels right now. Wiggle your toes and fingers, stretch and open your eyes when you're ready.

12. Remember to take your time and make sure that you feel completely safe and comfortable back in the room before you try to move.

Meditation in everyday life

Take some time to think about how you relax, especially those things that you can focus on without really thinking too much. Then spend fifteen minutes or so doing whatever that is.

As you do it, really focus – what can you hear, see and smell in this moment? How do you feel when you're doing this? Enjoy those positive feelings, and the happiness they bring you.

Daydream

Again, take some time out to daydream; set aside a period of time in which you can create your own perfect scenario. Whether it be a place you'd like to go, a thing you'd like to be or someone you would like to meet. As the story plays out in your mind, allow yourself to imagine all the details – how it sounds, feels; what you can see, even what you can smell, and really try to immerse yourself in that situation.

Let your mind and your imagination take you on a journey and relax as you enjoy being part of that journey.

Chapter Eight

How do you know when you're sensing Spirit?

It's great to know about Spirit and how to get in touch with them, but when it really gets down to it, how do you know when you're sensing the Spirit world and what should you expect when you open up to work with them?

If you've had contact with Spirit throughout your life, the chances are that you'll experience a lot of the same as you've already had. Contact from the Spirit world may come through clearer and more often once you invite them to work with you though and because of that, contact from them will probably start to make more sense.

When Spirits first try to get our attention they can do all sorts like playing with lights and other electrical items and hiding or moving things. Often when you start to work with the Spirit world these things calm down a bit, because they already have your attention. If they don't think you're listening they might still play the odd trick from time to time to catch your attention, but generally once you open yourself up to become a medium, working with the Spirit world becomes a lot calmer!

Starting out as a medium I was terrified about what I would see, hear, feel and experience when I opened myself up. What if a Spirit started to shout at me, or suddenly popped into my bedroom out of nowhere and woke me up? In my experience though, it's never been that terrifying...

How it feels

The first thing I generally notice when Spirits are around is that the air feels different – somehow calmer but also as though it is buzzing a bit. Inside too though, I tend to feel much calmer when

Spirits are around me and although they don't necessarily get rid of my fear, sadness, anger or anything else I might have been feeling, they do help me to see things more clearly and to feel better. Sometimes, if Spirits come in especially close they can leave me feeling excited and giddy to the point of seeming a little bit drunk. If you find yourself feeling that way it's especially important to make sure you're grounded and back to normal before you try to move about.

Like a lot of people who are sensitive to the Spirit world I've come across unhappy or less-than-light Spirits who have made me scared. Generally those energies bring a similar buzz to the air but it feels much colder and less pleasant. It's hard to describe but I guess it's the same as when you see someone and just know that they are going to cause trouble. More negative Spirits can also make me feel sick or give me a headache, both of which are signs for me to focus on protection, take a step back and ask the Spirits to back off a little too.

Hearing voices

As I've said already, hearing Spirit doesn't always mean actually hearing someone or something out loud. Hearing Spirit can be strange at first because it is literally a case of having someone else's voice inside your own mind, and often that voice isn't even one you recognise!

What's often even scarier than the idea of hearing dead people talk in your mind though is the idea that you might be hearing voices that aren't there, something lots of us are brought up to believe is wrong or means we're mentally ill. And of course, if you are constantly hearing voices that make you uncomfortable, or that are telling you to do something dangerous, then it's a good idea to talk to someone because Spirits who come from the light would *never* suggest you do anything that would hurt yourself or someone else.

But hearing Spirit isn't just about hearing voices, sometimes you might hear a song, piece of music or another sound that seems to pop up in your mind and stay there for no reason. Of course this happens sometimes if we really like a song, or if we've heard it on the TV or radio before we go to bed or when we first wake up. But when those noises seem to appear from nowhere, with no logical reason for you thinking of them, then they may be part of a message from Spirit.

That's not to say that you will never hear voices, music or other sounds out loud though. I tend to find that the difference between hearing the Spirit world out loud and hearing noises from the physical world is that Spirits sound quieter, or come and go quickly enough to cause me to wonder if I really heard it. If you've ever been somewhere and been sure you heard someone call your name, only to turn around and realise there was no one there, you'll know exactly what I mean! Because the Spirit world exists on a different frequency to ours, sometimes their voices and other noises can sound faster and higher-pitched than ours, almost like chipmunk voices! If that's what you hear don't worry, the more you practice opening up and raising your own vibrations, the more normal and easy to understand they will sound.

Seeing things

When it comes to seeing Spirit, I started out seeing things in my mind's eye rather than physically. Often that meant seeing people, animals or other images as though I was imagining them, but with no idea of where they've come from! The other difference between seeing Spirit in my mind's eye and my own imagination is that images from Spirit make absolutely no sense to me; which usually means they're messages for someone else!

When it comes to physically seeing the Spirit world it's pretty rare that they will actually pop up out of nowhere or hide around a corner waiting to scare you senseless. Usually Spirits are much more shy in making themselves seen! Often one of the first ways that you will see the Spirit world physically is out of the corners of your eyes; you might catch a glimpse of a shadow or sparkle but when you look again it will be gone.

The next step is physically seeing the Spirit world but not in quite the same way you see living breathing people and physical objects. A little while back before a big day at my work, I took a few minutes to call in all of the helpers and Angels I could think of to help things go smoothly. As I was sitting outside thinking and praying, I very clearly saw a face form on the grass in front of me. My first reaction was to blink and think I was imagining it but no, it was there – a very clear Spirit face in the grass in front of me.

And don't forget lights; Spirits often show themselves as balls or flashes of light that seem to appear from nowhere. I know one amazing medium who has seen Spirit lights for years and can even talk to and pick up messages from the way that they look and move.

I've never seen a fully formed Spirit person that I recognised as definitely being from the Spirit world, although that's not to say that I've never physically seen Spirit. Looking back, I honestly believe I've come across walking, talking Spirit people at least twice; in both cases they looked like every other person you might see, except that no one else seemed to be able to see them!

Other senses

Just like your other spiritual senses, often the easiest way to tell that you are smelling or tasting Spirit is because those sensations seem to come from nowhere and, in the case of smells, you're either the only person nearby or one of only a few people who can smell that scent.

When it comes to physically feeling Spirit, there are two main ways that the Spirit world will make themselves known to you; the first is by actually touching you, and when that happens it feels very like when a physical person or animal touches you, although sometimes it may feel unusually cold or especially warm. Of course though, the biggest giveaway is that it will feel as though you're being touched, but without anyone or anything physically touching you. That can be pretty strange and a bit scary at first but remember that, as long as you're protected, no one from the Spirit world will ever be able to come close enough to hurt you.

The other way that Spirits make themselves known physically could be by 'giving you' physical conditions to pass on to someone else. When that happens you might start to feel pain, tingling or some other sensation in a particular part of your body. If a feeling comes from out of nowhere when you start working with Spirit, then disappears quickly, then it is probably being 'put onto you' by the Spirit world, but remember that you should always talk to someone or see a doctor if you have a physical problem that doesn't go away.

Dreams

One of the easiest ways Spirits have to communicate with us is through dreams, maybe because we are at our most relaxed so it's easier for our energy to move more in tune with the Spirit world. But dreams can be pretty cool and magical at the best of times, so how do you tell if your dream is just a normal adventure from your imagination and your experiences from the day, or if it is the Spirit world saying hello?

Often Spirit dreams are super vivid; I have quite vivid dreams at the best of times but Spirit dreams, like the one I had about my nanna, are something else!

Another way to recognise dreams that come from Spirit is that they often include very important information which makes you wake up feeling as though you know exactly what to do next about a problem or situation. That's not to say though that every dream that makes you feel better has come from Spirit... Sometimes you just need to take credit for the fact that you knew the right answer all along!

The third sign you've had an experience with Spirit rather than an ordinary dream is when you wake up feeling very refreshed, and as though you've just been on a great adventure, but with no real idea of what the adventure involved. Sometimes Spirits bring us healing and information in dreams that they couldn't tell us when we were awake, because we wouldn't believe them. In those cases they will give us the information in our dreams, but so that we will forget the details once we wake up.

Animals around you

One almost surefire way to tell if there are Spirits around you is by watching any animals who are nearby. Animals are naturally excellent mediums, because their vibrations are higher than ours and because they have never had anyone tell them that they can't see or hear Spirit!

Dogs and cats are especially good at noticing the Spirit world and often watch a particular area, or grumble at what to us looks to be nothing because they see or hear things that we don't.

My dog, Kali, has been amazing at this since she was tiny. She often walks over to an empty chair in my house and sits in front of it tilting her head from side to side as though someone were talking to her. I have to admit, it was pretty weird at first, even for me, but now we're all used to it, and quite often ask her who she's talking to. The best thing about Kali's reaction to Spirit is that she sees Spirit people no differently to physical people, so we can always tell the difference between her reaction to someone that she knows like a guide or a family member, someone new that she's not familiar with, or (although it doesn't happen often) someone that she's scared of and not comfortable having around her family.

If you do have a dog, cat or other pet, prepare for them to possibly act a little differently when you start working with

Spirit but remember that's nothing to be scared or worried about, it can actually be a great help in trying to learn more about the Spirits around you.

Messages as they come through

Often Spirits come to you not just to say hello but to pass on a particular message that is meant for someone else (or sometimes for you, although that doesn't happen quite as often as you'd think!). When you first start working with Spirit and are trying to pass a message on to someone, it can be difficult to know for certain that information is coming from Spirit and not from your own imagination.

One of the easiest ways to spot a message for someone else is that the message means little or nothing to you, and seems a bit garbled. In those cases you will be amazed at how many of the tiny details that seem completely meaningless will mean so much to other people

As messages are coming through the information you receive can often leave you feeling quite emotional. That's not to say that they will make you cry or shout, but many messages will make you feel quite emotional because of the impact they will have on the people they're meant for. That could leave you feeling calm, happy or excited just as much as it could make you sad.

Lastly, and probably most commonly, the best way to spot a message from Spirit compared to your own imagination is because the messages that come through to you will use words, phrases or images that you wouldn't usually use. I'll often find, for example, that messages I give will use quite old-fashioned words or sayings, and if I'm writing from Spirit the way I write is often very different, with longer sentences and some very strange ways of saying things. It's important never to give messages until you're ready and comfortable though, but more on that later.

Protection

However you experience Spirit don't forget that you can always ask for or work on extra protection anytime you feel uncomfortable or unhappy about what you are experiencing.

And remember that you are within your rights to ask a Spirit to step back from you or to take a particular experience away if it is making you uncomfortable. You should never allow the Spirit world to scare you or make you feel uncomfortable in any way so call on your Guides or Angels for help any time you are struggling with this.

Chapter Nine

Meeting and working with your Guides

Almost any book you read about working with Spirit will mention Spirit Guides and there are lots of different ideas out there about who Guides are and what they do. In this chapter we'll look at the different types of Guides we each have and what their jobs are as well as how to meet and work with your Guides.

What are Guides?

Guides or Spirit Guides are Spirits whose job is to help and guide you on your journey through life. Some work with you from the second you choose to come here to Earth until the moment you go back to the Spirit world, while others will pop in and out of your life at particular times to help you with certain jobs, lessons or problems.

Many people believe that the little voice you may hear telling you to do something in particular, or not to do something dangerous, is the voice of your Guide, while others believe that your Guides act as gatekeepers or protectors, stopping other Spirits from coming too close to you and helping you to only work with those Spirits you are comfortable with. I sort of agree with both of those things, although I believe that our Guides do more than that too, and that each of us have plenty of other helpers in the Spirit world who can also do those things for us. The difference between our Guides and the other helpers is that Guides look after us especially and, because of that, know us better than anyone.

One of the nicest things about Spirit Guides in my opinion is that their job is to help one single person, meaning that our Guides are (for the most part) like our spiritual best friends. Like all Spirits, Guides can be in multiple places at once so can also work with, help or visit other souls both here and on the Other Side too, but their job is to look after you and only you and help you through life in the best way they can!

Who are your Guides?

From my experience we choose our Guides from two different groups of souls; those who have been friends or family members of ours in the past but who have agreed to help us from the Spirit world instead this time around. The second group are ascended or experienced Spirits who use everything they have picked up during their many, many lifetimes to help another soul on their journey through life – think of them as very good, very experienced teachers.

I believe that we choose most of our Guides long before we are born, and for that reason a lot of them aren't people we've known during this lifetime; of course those people help and support us from the Spirit world too but they do that alongside their own jobs on the Other Side.

That's not to say though that family members who passed into Spirit before we were born don't act as Guides for us, often great grandparents and other older relatives act as Ancestral Guides, helping us from Spirit in the way parents, grandparents and other relatives do here on Earth.

Most of our Guides are Spirits we have never known in this lifetime and don't consciously know anything about, although we may have known them since much further back than our physical memories can remember.

A lot of people see their Guides as traditionally wise figures such as monks, Native Americans, or priests and priestesses. I once knew an older medium who thought that Guides like that were just clichés and that no one really had them but I think that's a load of rubbish! Often the souls who choose to act as Guides are ones that have lived many lifetimes before, and since Spirits can make themselves appear anyway they choose wouldn't it make sense for them to present themselves in either the way you would recognise them from a past life or in the most wise-looking way possible?

If we all have Guides then why can life be so hard?

Wouldn't it be nice if our Guides could just keep us away from anything hard, nasty or painful? And hey, if their job is to look after us then why don't they just guide us through an easy life?!

Don't forget that life on Earth is all about learning and growing, and unfortunately we often learn the biggest lessons from the toughest and scariest things we come across. If our Guides moved us away from all of those situations then we would never learn the lessons they were bringing us and would have wasted all those opportunities to learn and grow.

That's not to say our Guides can't help us through those difficult times and situations though. By asking for their help and support and more importantly listening to what they have to say we can use our Guides' experience and wisdom, as well as our own, to help tackle the difficult situations we come across. And even when it seems that no one can help us through something, the important thing to remember is that your Guides are always with you so you never have to deal with anything alone.

New Guides

Some people think that each of us only has one Guide but that's definitely not the case. Every person on Earth has a group of Guides, each of which has a specific job to do. For example, as well as the Guides who help and guide us through life we all have specific Guides for our individual jobs and roles, such as healing Guides, mediumship Guides, writing Guides, teaching Guides or creative Guides.

Although some Guides are with you throughout the whole of your life, some come in and out as and when you need them to help with particular lessons you have ahead of you, particular jobs you have to do or particular parts of your life. For example when I went travelling a few years ago, I welcomed in a whole group of new Guides who helped me through my trip. Some of those Guides stayed with me long after I'd come home, but there are others that I've barely seen since I've been back. Many people also welcome in new Guides at different stages of their life such as when they leave school or when they have children.

If a Guide stops working closely with you that doesn't mean that you can never work with them again, many of them will still drop in from time to time to say hello and help you out but, in the same way you sometimes grow apart from friends, over time you will find that it becomes less important to see and work with your old Guides as much as you once did.

Guardian Angels

One particular type of helper that comes to us from the Spirit world is our Guardian Angel. Guardian Angels aren't technically Spirit Guides because they're Angels rather than normal Spirits, but they do have a lot in common with our Guides.

For starters Guardian Angels sign up to work with us before we even decide to come to Earth and agree to do that job for the whole of our lifetime, or even for many lifetimes.

A Guardian Angel's job is also similar to a Guide's because they're there to look after us and help keep us on the right path. The difference between the two types of helper though is that, as beings of pure love, our Guardian Angels want nothing more than to give us lots of love and positivity. Again, that doesn't mean that they'll stop us from ever experiencing anything unpleasant, but they will be there to provide spiritual hugs, comfort and help all the way through even the darkest of times.

Totems

Another type of Guide that each of us has is our Totem, or Animal Guide. The easiest way to describe Totems is as animal versions of Spirit Guides, but in the same way that pets are more special than just animal friends, Totems are much more than that.

Our Totems provide us with comfort, help, guidance, love, protection and also bring their own special qualities. For example, a horse Totem might bring you strength and steadiness or a dog might bring you courage and loyalty. Many people have a Totem animal with qualities similar to theirs, but for others their Totem seems to represent the complete opposite of them and the type of person they would like to be. I don't think that's true, maybe it's just that your Totem represents the real you that you haven't yet uncovered!

I often think of Totems as being a bit like the daemons in Philip Pullman's *His Dark Materials* books and the patronuses in Harry Potter; the animal parts of our soul that not only represent and protect us but who grow and develop with us right the way through our lives.

I once read about a woman who recognised her Totem because people told her that they had seen a big cat sitting on her windowsill every night, even though she didn't have a cat in her house. Similarly I had a friend who would often wake up and see a big fish swimming around his room; eventually he realised he was seeing his Totem – a shark. But how do you recognise your own Totem?

Often your Totem will be an animal that you are particularly drawn to or feel like you have a link to; I have a friend who loves elephants but has no idea why. I don't know for certain because she's not particularly interested in spiritual things, but I'm convinced that her Totem is an elephant.

Sometimes it's exactly the opposite – your Totem may be an animal that you are frightened or wary of, or especially uncomfortable around. For example, my Totem is a big cat – a leopard I think – which suits me pretty well. But I've never been a big fan of cats. In fact cats generally hate me! Over the years though I've come to realise that a lot of that is because of my Totem; normal cats don't like me because they're scared of the huge cat that prowls around with me, understandable really!

One thing is for certain though, no one type of Totem is any better or any worse than another. Every living creature is just as special and important as the next, and every species has important qualities to bring to the world. So whether your Totem is a spider, a tiger, a dog or a brontosaurus, you can rest assured that it is perfect for you and will bring you everything you need from it for this lifetime.

If you have no idea about what your Totem might be then don't worry. At the end of this chapter is a meditation to put you in touch with your Totem and, the more open-minded you are going into that, the more information you're likely to get. So give it a go and see what you find out.

Elemental Guides

Elementals are nature Spirits whose purpose is to look after the natural world and to spread the beautiful qualities of nature to everyone and everything they come in contact with. They come in various different groups depending on the elements, plants or other creations that they belong to (including, according to many people, our own physical bodies) and, like other Spirits, can appear in whatever forms they wish so may look like flashes of light, colours, or even more traditional Elemental figures such as faeries, gnomes or sylphs – although I can't say I've personally seen a fully formed Elemental yet, no matter how much I'd like to!

As natural beings each of us has our own Elementals whose jobs are to bring us back in touch with the natural world, and to help us maintain a balance between all of the Elements around us and the qualities that they represent.

The easiest way to come into contact with your Elementals is to head outdoors and get as close to the natural world as you can. It's not always easy or safe to go through your usual opening-up routine outdoors but even just sitting quietly, protecting yourself and asking your Elementals to step forward and talk to you is fine.

You may not see or hear anything different but pay attention to your energy levels and to how you feel as your nature Guides draw close to you. Call on your Elementals for help whenever you're feeling tired, unwell or out of balance in some way. Unlike many other Spirits your Elementals can also help if you're struggling to ground yourself.

Recognising and working with your Guides

When I first started working with Spirit it bothered me that I didn't know who my Guides were, or how to recognise them, because it seemed as though every other medium out there could name and describe their Guides perfectly, while I didn't have a clue.

Since then though I've realised that's not quite true! Although some mediums see and hear their Guides perfectly and have great relationships with them, others (like me) work with their Guides without ever really getting to know them well. However, over time I have come to recognise my Guides and to know what each of them is there to help me with and how best to work with them.

The easiest way to recognise and get to know your Guides is through meditations like the one at the end of this chapter. If you're not particularly comfortable with meditation though, often it's just as easy to get to know your Guides simply by paying attention and by sitting quietly and asking them to step forward.

Also, pay attention to the way you feel and the impressions you get when you do certain things. For a long time, when I opened up to work with Spirit I would feel a long ponytail on the back of my head, even when my hair was tucked up or loose down my back. Over time I recognised the ponytail belonged to a Japanese warrior who would stand and protect me every time I opened up to the Spirit world.

A good friend of mine is an amazing spiritual healer, but for ages I couldn't properly relax when she was working near me because I would hear loud laughing and see a skeleton face...pretty freaky! It took a bit of listening, watching and waiting but we realised eventually that her healing Guide is a voodoo healer. And although he's pretty scary to look at, he's not really that way at all.

Your own Guides will have their own ways of making themselves known to you. So watch and listen out when you open up to do a particular type of Spiritual work and see what impressions you get. When it comes to your generic Guides trust your intuition; what type of person or historical period jumps out at you when you think about your Guides? When you sit quietly and ask them to step forward, what impressions do you get? Trust the feelings that come to you and remember that your Guide is incredibly close to you, and you already know them better than anyone, whether you realise it or not.

Meeting your Guides

1. Sit or lie comfortably somewhere where you won't be disturbed for at least fifteen minutes. Close your eyes, breathe deeply and try to clear your mind as you concentrate on the rhythm of those breaths;

2. Protect yourself and open up as usual then allow yourself to sit for a moment in this beautiful spiritual energy as you continue to concentrate on your breathing;

3. As you breathe, imagine yourself in front of a beautiful doorway. As you look at the door in front of you know that this is your doorway; placed here especially for you to lead you to somewhere that is safe and special to you;

4. When you're ready, head through that door and into a

beautiful room on the other side. As you look around pay attention to the details of this room and again, recognise that this room is yours – a safe and beautiful place intended just for you;

5. As you sit calmly, enjoying the beautiful energy of your room, feel someone else come in. As you feel another energy in the room know that other person is here to love and support you;

6. Look at the other figure in the room and recognise this person as one of your Guides. As you look at them, try and take in as much information about them as you can, and pay attention to other details too – do they bring a particular smell? How do you feel when they are near you? Pay attention to those feelings and to your other senses as you feel them with you;

7. Your Guide steps forward and greets you, introducing themselves to you. They may give you a name or give you other impressions about them. Pay attention to the information they give you and to any feelings you have alongside these;

8. Ask the Spirit in front of you for their guidance or advice, either about a particular subject that's been bothering you or for some general guidance they may wish to bring you, and then take a few moments to listen to whatever they want to tell you.

9. Ask your Guide to bring forward other Guides who are working with you at this time. If anyone else comes forward pay attention to them and the impressions they bring you in same way as you did before.

10. Once your Guides have introduced themselves together you head outside to a beautiful outdoor space where there is an animal waiting for you;

11. Whatever animal is waiting for you don't be afraid or wary. Know that this is your Totem and is here just for

you, again to protect, guide and support you, and carrying an energy of pure love just for you;

12. Pay attention to the animal in front of you; what kind of animal is it, what colour is it, what size is it? Again pay attention to how your Totem makes you feel and to how you can recognise their energy around you;

13. Allow your Totem to draw close to you and pay attention to the feelings it gives you and the impressions you get with it. Look into your Totem's eyes and, if you're both willing, reach out and touch it;

14. Spend a few moments with your Totem picking up any wisdom it wants to share with you or any qualities it wants to pass on to you;

15. Once your Totem has passed on all that it needs to, thank both of your Guides for their time and wisdom;

16. Say goodbye to your Guides, taking away any last impressions or words of wisdom that they have for you and then step back from them;

17. As you say goodbye know that, although you may be leaving your Guides behind in this place, they are always with you and will be with you wherever you go, keeping you safe and supporting you throughout your life. Know also that you can come back here to this safe and wonderful place anytime you wish either to see your Guides or to spend time alone somewhere safe and calm;

18. Allow your spiritual self to close your eyes and enjoy this beautiful place for a few more moments before focusing on your breathing once again;

19. As you concentrate on your breathing, bring your attention back to the physical again – become aware of the sensations of your physical body as it comes back to your awareness, and of the room around you – take notice of the temperature, of what you can hear and smell, and of anything else you feel around you;

20. Focus wholly on your body and bring yourself back completely to the physical world; stretch, wiggle your fingers and toes and do whatever else you need to bring yourself back completely. Then, when you're ready, open your eyes and come back into the room.

Chapter Ten

Developing your connection

I know I'm biased but working and communicating with Spirit is one of the coolest things I've ever done and means I can help people in ways I only ever dreamed of doing. That said though, when I first started out as a medium I wasn't so confident.

How could I ever know that I was really a medium and wasn't just imagining everything I thought I experienced? And how could I be sure the Spirits who were talking to me were the good ones who were honest and serious and meant me no harm?

There's no simple way of answering those questions. In fact, the only way to really know for sure is to test our connection and keep testing and working on it until we have complete faith not just in our abilities but in our Guides and the information that they allow to come through to us from Spirit.

The simplest way to do this is to ask for proof from the Spirit world of the information that they are giving you. Although I'm not suggesting that you ask them for the winning lottery numbers (as lovely as that would be) or for proof of exactly how your day is going to pan out, there is no harm at all in asking for them to give you something that you can use as a small piece of proof.

Sit quietly and talk to the Spirit world – explain that you are trying to develop your connection with them further so that you can trust the information you're given and be the best medium you can possibly be. Then ask them to give you something to act as proof. And once you have your evidence to look out for don't just sit back and wait – go look for it! Go out there and live life for the day or the week, or whatever timescale you've given, but keep your eyes open and wait for that proof to roll in.

I don't know about you but I'm pretty impatient when it

comes to waiting for things that I want or have asked for. However, one of the biggest things I've learned about the Spirit world over the years is that time really doesn't mean anything to them. So by all means give timescales when you're asking for your sign. But if that's the case, don't be upset if your sign arrives a little late; it doesn't mean that they aren't with you, just that they're not quite so impatient as we are!

Signs from Spirit

When it comes to asking for proof from Spirit you can ask for pretty much anything that you want. However, there are some well-known common signs that Spirit is around you and it's nice to be able to recognise them not only when you've asked for them but any time, just as a little reminder that Spirit is with you.

Some of the most common signs are:

- Feathers: A lot of people know that white feathers are a sign that Angels are around, but feathers in general can be signs that Spirit is with you;
- Butterflies: Butterflies are often signs from Spirit, especially when they come particularly close or appear at times when you wouldn't usually see them;
- Birds: Again, birds coming particularly close or appearing at odd times can often be a sign that Spirit is with you;
- Clouds: Lying back watching clods can be very relaxing and is a great way to meditate if you're struggling. But Spirit also likes to send messages to us in the form of clouds that are certain shapes. In particular look out for Angel clouds, bird clouds, spaceship clouds and butterfly clouds;
- Shooting stars: Spirit will sometimes send us a little hello in the form of shooting stars. They may not be quite so common as other signs but I sometimes think they're extra special – a hello from Spirit with the opportunity to make a wish attached!

And of course there are much less natural, but equally special signs from Spirit. I've lost track of the number of times I've seen the signs or answers I've just asked Spirit for on the backs of lorries, in car number plates or on posters. Remember that when it comes to signs and hellos from Spirit there's no such thing as coincidence.

Your own signs

Spirits work with every medium differently, and one of the most individual ways that they work with us is through the language and signs they give us.

I used to know a medium who regularly gave messages from and about members of the armed forces. I give the odd message from a soldier who has passed away, but it seemed as though every single message this guy gave included at least one military person. It helped that he had an interest in military history, so whenever someone came through in uniform he could not only tell the person which service they were in but could go as far as telling their rank and sometimes even their regiment (far better than me, who just about manages to identify a Spirit as a soldier who might be from the First World War!).

I know other mediums who are keen gardeners, or big dog lovers, and almost always give out plants or animals within the messages they pass on. And then there are other people whose "codes" from Spirit have nothing to do with their own interests but regularly include things like colours or pieces of music.

For me, there are a few really common signs that I often get within the messages that they pass on; things that seem random but which come through so often I now have a good idea of what Spirits are trying to say when they ask me to refer to them.

Many people will tell you that certain things you're given as a medium have set meanings which you need to pass on but I don't believe that. An older medium I knew would regularly try and do this with me; for example I'd tell someone I saw blue around them and she'd shout: "That means healing." Actually, no, to me it doesn't, and maybe to the person sending or receiving the message it doesn't either.

I'm not suggesting you should never use the traditional definitions of things; it's always a good idea to take advice and ideas on board from other people. But when it comes to interpreting messages don't take what anyone else says as definite; take what feels right for you and then ignore the things that don't seem to fit. And if you need to ask someone how to understand the messages that you're given then ask your Guides, they will always give you the right answer.

Give a message

Maybe one of the biggest ways to build your connection and convince yourself of your own abilities is to pass on a message to someone from Spirit. But when it comes to doing this for the first time, or the first few times, only ever give messages when you feel ready, comfortable and are in the right situation (and after you've read the next chapter!).

The first time I gave someone a message from Spirit was in a spiritualist church I'd been going to for a few weeks. I was absolutely terrified! I remember standing up thinking: "What if I've just made this up? What if this makes no sense to anyone? What if I'm not really talking to Spirit and I'm just mad?" Guess what, none of those things turned out to be true.

Passing on a message from Spirit for the first time can be really scary because it means putting your complete trust into someone or something else and risking looking silly. However, how will you ever be able to fully trust your connection with Spirit unless you test it, and unless the information that you've been given is verified by someone else?

If you don't want to go to a spiritualist church then ask a friend who you know is interested in spiritual matters to sit for you and allow you to try to give them a message. Make sure you ask someone you trust but try to ask someone whose family and background you don't know too much about. Then sit quietly with them, open up and see what information comes.

Connecting with Spirit is always easiest when you're relaxed, although I know that's easier said than done when you're first starting out. I've found that one of the easiest ways to gain information from the Spirit world is by talking to and about them – maybe say a prayer or ask the Angels to help you pass on the most perfect healing and guidance to the soul in front of you before you open up, then if nothing comes through straight away talk a little about what you believe and why.

Don't be afraid to start small

Remember even the smallest pieces of information are important. In fact, for some people a particular word or image can be more important than the longest and most complicated message they've ever been given.

During my first visit back to church after I'd been travelling, a man stood up to give me a message and looked very frustrated. "I'm so sorry," he said, "I have a message for you but I only have one little thing and it makes no sense, but I can't get anything else! All I have for you is an animal that looks like a llama, but I'm being told that it's not a llama, it's something else. I'm sorry."

I laughed out loud and told that man to please stop apologising...less than two weeks before I'd trekked the Inca Trail in Peru for charity, in memory of my granddad who had passed away earlier that year. Although I'd heard and felt my granddad with me throughout the trek, I'd been desperate for someone else to confirm that he'd been with me. So how was this the confirmation I'd been looking for? Well right along the Inca Trail are alpacas, which look very very similar to llamas!

In the years since I've had lots of messages from my granddad, and they've all been special and very welcome. But that one little alpaca still remains one of the most special messages that any medium has ever given me. So never feel that any message is too small for you to get up and give. Often more information will come through from Spirit as soon as you start to pass a message on, but even if that's not the case then remember, even the smallest of details could mean the world to the person you're talking to.

Feeling alone

One of my favourite things about being a medium is that I never have to feel lonely, because I know I'm never on my own. But that's not to say that the Spirit world will always be at your beck and call anytime you want them. Sometimes they back off a little, never because they are abandoning you or leaving you alone, but often because it's time for you to learn some particular lessons about yourself, like how strong you really are.

An old medium once told me that every medium goes through at least one period of having their faith tested, where they go to work with Spirit and the information just doesn't flow, meaning that they have to work really hard to make any sort of sense of what they're given, or even just to get anything at all! At the time I was just starting out and thought: "Pft, as if my Guides and helpers would ever do that to me!" Well guess what...about six months later that's exactly what they did.

I would go into church, stand up to give messages and get nothing, or get a load of garbled information that seemed to make no sense to anyone. This went on for about two months, and I would walk out at the end of those nights having some very stern words with my Guides. But as you can imagine, they didn't say much in return! There were a few times during that period, and the next period of quiet, that I thought about giving up or wondered if maybe I wasn't a very good medium after all. But during all of those times something (probably my own stubbornness!) always made me give it another go. After a few weeks each period of struggling would come to an end and, almost every time Spirit would not only come back to work with me again I'd find that my connection was even stronger than it had been before.

Sometimes the problems may not be your connection with Spirit, but with the physical people you are talking to. In those cases it can be easy to think you must be wrong, and give up on passing the message on, but if I've learned one thing about developing my connection with the Spirit world it's how important it is to have faith in the information that they send you.

My favourite example of that is the woman I asked to please be careful when she was reversing out of the drive because I could see her running over a cat. She was absolutely adamant that she couldn't understand that, and after a few minutes of her saying no I decided it was probably best to just give up. At the end of the evening I was getting ready to leave when she came over to me and said: "You know the message you gave about the cat? Well I don't know if it's linked but as I was pulling off the drive tonight I backed into my cat – she's fine but it gave me a really big fright," then proceeded to run through everything else she'd said no to and ask if maybe I could've been talking about certain things and people that were exactly as I'd described!

Sometimes it's because they're scared, sometimes because they're embarrassed, and sometimes because when they're put on the spot their minds go blank, but living people are often the hardest part of mediumship! So if you find yourself giving a message to someone who doesn't seem to understand any of it, don't automatically blame your connection with Spirit.

On those occasions, I usually ask Spirit for more information; if that doesn't work and I'm certain that I'm definitely talking to the right person, I'll usually either give them what I have and ask them to just think about it when they get home, or will offer to talk to them at the end, just in case anything does make sense to them.

Remember that the Spirit world never leaves you, and that every person out there is capable of having a perfectly clear connection with them. So even when it feels as though they're not with you don't give up, it probably means that there's something important for you to learn from your current situation.

Chapter Eleven

Being a responsible medium

If you're a geek like me you'll remember Peter Parker's (Spiderman) Uncle Ben telling him that with great power comes great responsibility. I'm not saying that being a medium is anything like having super powers but I've always thought it was a good motto for working with the Spirit world.

Although I believe that everyone can communicate with Spirit if they want to, a lot of people don't see it that way. And when you start talking to the Other Side or passing messages on from their loved ones some people will look up to you as being something pretty special.

One of the most important lessons to learn about being a medium is how to keep your ego in check when it comes to that sort of reaction. Because although it's lovely to have people say how special and important you are, it can be easy to let praise like that go to your head, and once that happens the most important part of being a good medium – your intention to do good – can very easily go a bit wrong and some of the wrong reasons can start to creep in instead.

I've always thought that being a medium – and especially being able to help people by passing messages on from the Other Side – is a real honour and it's important to learn how to live up to that responsibility and be the best medium you can be, not just to keep yourself safe but also for the sake of the people you are working with on both sides of life.

The first and most important thing to remember when it comes to passing on messages from Spirit is that many people you talk to will be grieving and suffering, so it's important to be as sensitive and as honest as you can possibly be.

I know I sound like a loser, but bad mediums are one of my

pet hates! So here are what I think are the five golden rules for passing on messages from Spirit. Some of these might sound like common sense, but you'd be amazed at how many supposedly good mediums ignore them, or don't even consider these things in the work that they do.

The five golden rules of passing on messages from Spirit

1. Don't fish

There is nothing less convincing than a medium who fishes for information, and since one of a medium's jobs nowadays is to help prove that there is life after death, it's important to give as clear evidence as you can to help people recognise that they are actually receiving messages from the Other Side.

Fishing means asking questions; things like: "Is your mum in Spirit? Did she pass away in hospital?" It's one thing to ask the odd question to check that someone understands what you're telling them, but totally different to pass your whole message on through questions because then really who is giving who the message?

I once had a private sitting with a medium who started off with a load of questions about what I did for a living, who I had lost, whether I had a boyfriend or any brothers or sisters and all of our star signs. She gave me the most woolly message I've ever heard, peppered with the odd piece of information about me or the people I cared about...it was only after I left (having paid her) that I realised all of the details she'd given were things I'd already told her! And although some of the stuff she said was positive, she'd done so much fishing that I had to wonder whether she was just telling me what I wanted to hear.

The other extreme was an amazing tarot reading I once had; the lady talked to me for over an hour and asked about five questions in that whole time to check out my understanding of what she'd said, things like: "If I talked to you about a gentleman who passed away very recently – as in earlier this year – and was very confused before he passed into Spirit would you know who I was talking about?" That lady was amazing and I'm not suggesting you need to have that much detail before you ask any checking out-type questions, but hopefully you can see the difference between the two types of question and how much of a difference they can make to the person hearing the messages.

2. Don't state the obvious

This more than any other "rule" can be tough at times. After all, if you have some information to pass on from Spirit then surely you should pass it on, even if it does sound a bit obvious? And yes, to a point that's true, but the key is to give as much detail as you can without just saying what is obviously going to be true.

Say you have a lady with a baby bump sitting in front of you, it would be silly to say "I'm being shown there's new life coming for you"...no, really? Although there's no harm in mentioning her bump if it's part of the message. Similarly, if you have a very old lady in front of you then saying "Your grandmother is in Spirit" is probably obvious, but describing the lady who is talking to you and saying that she comes in with a very grandmotherly feeling gives more detail. Remember, it's important to prove that these messages are coming from Spirit, otherwise why should they listen?

3. Don't be mean or rude

I know it sounds obvious but passing on messages from Spirit is the same as any other conversation you have in that it's important to remember to treat others as you would like to be treated.

I know one medium who says exactly what he sees. I once

heard him stand in front of a room full of people and tell a lady that he was talking to her mother who hadn't been able to go to the toilet properly in the last years of her life. Even if that were right would you want a room full of people to know that your mum had been that way? And just as importantly, if you were that lady's mum is that how you would want someone to remember you? Even if that's how you see someone, there's always a kinder and more positive way to describe them; maybe mentioning that you get the impression they needed a lot of care towards the end of their life, or describing a bit more about how they look and the surroundings you see them in. Showing respect for the people you're dealing with on both sides of life is very important when it comes to passing on communication from the Spirit world, and it's something you can never do too much of.

4. Don't jump to conclusions

As I've mentioned already in this book, as a medium it's important to remember that something you interpret one way could mean something totally different to the person you're talking to.

I often see Big Ben in messages and although I go to London pretty regularly I don't often see Big Ben when I'm there, so that symbolises New Year more than anything. For other people though Big Ben is the biggest symbol of London there is.

Another more embarrassing example is a medium from the church I often go to who once told a room full of people (including my grandma, who was over the moon!) that I was pregnant, then spent the next five minutes telling me she was definitely right and I would have a baby very soon. Well, a year and a bit on I still don't have a baby, although I did get the opportunity shortly afterwards to write this book and "give birth" to something that had always been very important to me.

It's not always easy to know what Spirits are trying to say, particularly when they seem to talk in words and pictures that mean very little to you. But it's important to remember that you're often just the messenger who passes those messages on to someone who will understand them. The easiest way to do that is just to say what you see. You can add something else in there about what that means to you if you like; for example: "I'm being shown a picture of Big Ben. To me that usually means the New Year, but I don't know if Big Ben means something different to you."

If the person isn't sure, that's absolutely fine too – sometimes the messages we give mean nothing at first and it's only later that they come to understand them. However, I'm a firm believer that the first person or thing that springs to a person's mind (and gut) when they're given a message from Spirit is usually right.

5. Don't say anything scary or give bad news
For a lot of people communicating with the Spirit world is scary, especially if that involves talking to someone they didn't have the best relationship with or who was in a lot of pain before they passed into Spirit. For that reason, it's important to make sure that the messages you give aren't going to scare anyone.

For example, saying to someone like me that their granddad is around them and will make themselves known around the house may seem lovely. However, telling that to someone who is scared of the Spirit world and expects them to pop up in the sitting room, or whose granddad was an angry man, may be quite scary. One of the easiest ways around this is just to explain the message a little better, and to talk about the feelings behind it. If I'm telling someone that a person will be coming around their house, for example, I'll often point out to them that it's nothing to be frightened of, and that their granddad never wants to do anything that would scare or upset them, but that if ever the person is uncomfortable they just need to ask the Spirit to step back or go away altogether.

One of the oldest rules of mediumship is that you should never ever give bad news. It's important to remember that you can't necessarily see the future – partly because everyone can change their fate but also because, as we've already explained, it's very easy to misinterpret what Spirit is trying to tell you. I know someone who was told that her only daughter would die giving birth to her first grandchild. Fast forward over 20 years and when her daughter announced she was pregnant this lady spent nine months terrified that her daughter was going to die. Did she? Of course not! But then the mother worried that maybe she'd remembered the message wrongly...and when grandchild number two came along she worried herself sick all over again that it would be the second baby that killed her instead. Again, that didn't happen but the poor woman spent a long time dreading having grand-children and then wasn't even able to enjoy the excitement of becoming a grandma.

In my experience if your intention is right, you will rarely pick up bad news for people. However, on the odd occasion that does happen then it's the one type of information you should never pass on. After all, what if you have interpreted the message wrong or if the person you're talking to or about decides to do something which changes the way things are going to turn out?

By all means give out little words of warning like: "I'm being asked to tell you to drive more carefully,"; "Could you make sure the person who eats a lot of fatty foods gets a more balanced diet please?"; or "I'm getting the impression your great aunt needs a bit of help at the moment – could you give her a call or pop in to see her if possible please?"; but please don't give them any bad news associated with that guidance!

Sometimes in the heat of the moment, especially when you're nervous and just learning how to manage the information that's coming through to you from Spirit, it can be strangely difficult to follow all of the rules above and to give messages out in the most responsible way possible. But it's important to remember that you're never alone in this.

Ask for guidance and help, particularly from Archangel Haniel who is responsible for compassion, Archangel Raphael who is the healer of the Angels, and Archangel Gabriel who helps us to communicate clearly and confidently, and they will help you to be the most respectful medium you can be. Something as simple as the following before you start to give out any of the information you receive can work wonders:

"Archangel Haniel, please surround me with your beautiful light of compassion and help everything I say and do here to be said and done in the name of love and light. Archangel Raphael, help me to provide perfect healing on all levels for all those I speak to this evening both here in the physical world and in the Spirit realm. Archangel Gabriel, please help me to communicate with perfect clarity, confidence and love with all those I work with today on both sides of life."

When to pass on messages

When you first start working and communicating with the Spirit world, it can be easy to think that you should pass on messages from Spirits all the time whenever they come and speak to you. But it's important to remember that to just leap on someone with an unexpected message from their dead relative could be scary, upsetting, or could make them incredibly angry.

Only ever pass on messages with permission – and that generally doesn't mean walking up to someone in the street and saying: "Hi, I'm a medium and I have your dead auntie here, is it OK if I talk to you?" – it means waiting until you're somewhere like a spiritualist church or a psychic fair where that person has come because they're comfortable with the possibility of receiving a message from Spirit.

Even then it's important to remember that some people come to a medium before they're necessarily ready to hear from Spirit or, more often, from a particularly person that they're close to. If you're ever not comfortable giving a particular message to someone then it's fine to step back and ask the Spirit to go through another medium, and if you ever begin talking to someone who is clearly not ready to receive the message and either shuts down completely or gets very upset, then it's OK to offer to stop and to either talk to them privately at the end of any public session, or to just pass on the love of Spirit and leave it there. At times that can feel like you aren't doing your job properly but remember, the person will receive that message at the perfect time and from the perfect medium for them, while you will go on to give plenty more messages that help lots more people.

Whenever you give messages, it's equally important to keep yourself safe, and to make sure you don't try to work with Spirit when you're not ready or comfortable. Sometimes that means not pushing yourself and your mediumship further than you're comfortable with and learning how to say no to anyone who asks you to do more than you're happy with. At other times it's more about how you're physically feeling; if you're too tired, feeling ill or really upset about something then not only are you unlikely to be concentrating on being a good medium, but your protection will probably be lower than it should be too, so always take care of yourself first of all where mediumship is concerned.

Emotions

Passing messages to and from relatives who have passed into Spirit can be pretty emotional, and it's important to go easy on yourself and the people you're talking to.

At some point you will almost definitely pass on a message that makes someone particularly emotional, usually in terms of them crying, although they may get angry, hysterical or something else. If that happens, remember the respect we talked about earlier – would you like to be in tears front of a room full of people, or even just one person you don't know well?

I've found that the best way to deal with that is to ask the person if they want to continue – something like: "I can see that this is bringing up some really strong emotions for you. Do you want me to stop?" If you're somewhere public like a spiritualist church you can offer to talk to the person privately at the end, although if you choose to do that keep yourself safe and make sure there are still other people around when you do.

Sometimes the strong emotions you feel come from those you are talking to in Spirit. And that makes sense – it must be so frustrating not to be able to just talk to someone you love and to have to prove it's you who is speaking. Again, if Spirits come through to you with very strong emotions it's absolutely fine to ask them to step back, or to ask your Guides to help calm the emotions down a little so that the message is easier to understand and pass on.

Giving a very emotional message can have a real impact on your own feelings and emotions. Again, remember to keep yourself safe and to ask your Guides to help you step back from the message if you are at all uncomfortable. And remember to close down and ground yourself at the end of every session of working with Spirit just to bring you back to yourself and put you back in touch with your own feelings and emotions again.

How to give messages

If you watch other mediums give messages you'll find that the ways they do that are as different as the mediums themselves. Some will wave their arms about, others will stand completely still; some will seem to have full on conversations with the Spirits they're talking to, nod and tilt their heads as though they're listening intently, while others will just talk to you normally without any outward sign that anyone else is involved in the conversation.

As with everything related to Spirit work there's no right or wrong way to give a message in that respect. Do what feels right and comfortable for you and, as long as it doesn't involve being starkers in public or dancing the Macarena every time you try to give someone a message then you won't go far wrong.

Some places you go may ask you to stand or sit a certain way while you pass messages on; one church I went to insisted on mediums standing up unless for some reason they weren't able to, while one church chairperson I knew refused to let anyone who was giving a message walk away from the chair and into the centre of the circle we were all sitting in. Of course there are times you have to abide by the rules of wherever you are, but as with everything else don't do anything that makes you feel uncomfortable and don't feel that's the way you have to act elsewhere.

Some mediums behave in certain ways as though they're trying to act out their messages; waving their arms in the air, using different voices for the different Spirits they're talking to and making a big show of asking for more information for example. As with everything else, if that's what you want to do then that's up to you, but think about the image you're giving out by doing that. Acting like an entertainer can be great fun and put some people at ease, but it's not always the most credible thing if you're trying to prove without a shadow of a doubt that you're communicating with Spirit.

Alcohol

When it comes to drinking (or using any other sort of drug for that matter), there is an old saying that you should never mix the spirits, and that's an important message to remember.

I used to know a medium who told a story about a time he had been out for dinner and drinks when someone had mentioned that he was a medium. The group had egged him on to open up and give a message and eventually that's just what he did, picking up a message for one lady at the table he barely knew and telling her that she must be expecting a baby because he could see a lady in Spirit holding on to a baby and was sure that she was preparing that baby to come down to Earth. The lady he was speaking to went very quiet and left to go home shortly afterwards...it turned out that she and her husband had recently lost a baby to the Spirit world.

The other problem with opening up to the Spirit world after drinking is that your energies are all over the place, meaning that it's much easier to attract the wrong sort of Spirits. There are quite a few times when I've been out with friends and, since I was relaxed and my guard was lower than usual, opened up my energies without realising, only to find myself attracting some very odd characters (and not just the ones who were chatting me up!).

A lot of people will tell you that the most sensible thing to do if you work with Spirit is to never touch a single drop of alcohol, and there are lots of very good reasons for them to suggest that, but what you do and don't eat or drink is up to you. If you are going to drink then try to remember to put up your protection before you have your first sip, and please don't ever, ever try to work with Spirit after you've been drinking alcohol.

Money

And then we get to money...some mediums out there refuse to charge a penny for use of their abilities; others see it like any other sort of talent or skill and think that if they can make a living from what they're good at then why on earth wouldn't they; and then there are the third group, who talk about their special gifts, charge a lot for what they do and make a very healthy income from their work with Spirit.

Which one should you do? Well that's completely up to you, but here are a few pointers before you even think about charging anything for what you do.

First of all, as with anything that you're asking people to pay for, practice, practice, practice and don't even think about charging until you're not only good at what you do but are confident in your own abilities to communicate both with Spirit and with your physical customers.

While you are practicing, try as many different things as you can (there are some ideas later in this book) to see what your particular specialties might be and get as much experience as you can. If you choose to go to a spiritualist church or something similar every week that's great, but don't just stick to the same one; try out different churches so you can practice working with different energies and test yourself with new and different people.

When you do feel that you're a good enough medium to start thinking about charging, don't let anyone else talk you into it until it feels absolutely right for you and you feel that you're ready.

If and when you decide to start charging for your work with Spirit, how much do you charge? Again, the simple answer is that it's up to you, but I have a few words of advice. First of all, be fair to both yourself and the people you will be dealing with; remember that a lot of the people who will come to you for guidance or communication from Spirit will really be struggling, and to charge them a small fortune for your services can seem like you're taking advantage of them. My other advice would be to do some research; look at what other people who offer similar services to you are charging, and ask people that you know how much they would be willing to pay either for your services or for the services of someone like you.

Remember, if you're just starting out then you may not be able to charge as much as someone who has been doing the same thing for years. At the end of the day you're talking about starting a business, and any business has to build its reputation and customer base before it can expect to earn a lot of money. But remember also that what you're doing is work, so make sure you're being fair to yourself too.

Once you start charging for your services it gets a bit more complicated than just working with Spirit because it interests you. If someone pays you to do something then you have a duty to do it as well as you possibly can for them, and remember that if your business really takes off, or if you already have another job and are old enough to do so, you may also have to pay tax on what you earn.

There are also laws you need to abide by if you charge for any service. In the UK for example, the Consumer Protection Regulations say that anyone charging money for a product or service has to deliver exactly what they say they will. The difficulty with this is that communication with Spirit is still difficult to prove – particularly to someone who is a sceptic. There are ways to cover yourself with that, but be sure to look into them fully before you charge for anything.

Look after number one

I've said it before but I'll say it again because, as you might have gathered, I think it's pretty critical! The biggest responsibility you have when it comes to working with Spirit is to yourself.

Remember to protect, protect, protect, both for your own good and for the good of everyone around you; and remember to keep your intention as high and as positive as possible to make sure you're attracting the most positive energies and the best and clearest results possible. And remember that protecting yourself isn't just a spiritual thing, it also means never going anywhere alone to give messages, or meeting someone you don't know on your own, and always keeping yourself safe and well.

Chapter Twelve

Working in a way that's right for you

Working and communicating with the Spirit world is a very personal thing. And since a big and important part of mediumship is holding the right intention about what you're doing, it's very important that you listen to yourself and only ever work with Spirit in a way that's right for you.

Spiritual teachers

I have never been to a single spiritual development class. I've thought about it before, but most of the classes I found or was invited to were held on nights I couldn't commit to because of work, night classes or other commitments. And whenever I did find a class that fitted in with the rest of my life, they were run by teachers that just didn't feel right for me.

That's not to say it's not important to have an experienced medium helping you learn your trade when it comes to working with Spirit. I would never have developed as safely, confidently or quickly if it hadn't been for the lovely experienced mediums I befriended along my way who would encourage me, or give me pep talks and honest feedback at the end of a session; in my experience it's as important to have a physical teacher or guide when it comes to mediumship as it is to be in touch with your Spirit Guides and helpers.

The best teachers will be the ones who help, guide and support you, but allow you to do things your own way. The best teachers will help you to work safely and find the ways that are best for you, but will often just sit back and watch, ready to step up and help if you have any problems or worries.

Good spiritual teachers will never tell you you must do something, at least not unless it's to keep you safe, and not without a good explanation. They may suggest that you do a certain thing or encourage you to follow a certain path or procedure, but they will know that you have to do what feels right for you so will generally be quite comfortable if you try their idea but then decide that your way works much better for you.

Doing what feels right

Not long ago I was at a spiritualist church when the lady who runs their open circle asked if I had a message. I said I did, but since it was quite personal and emotional I wasn't prepared to give it in front of the circle and would catch that person after-wards instead. I was told that no, I would give the message there and then. The easiest thing to do would have been to stand up and give that message – just to shut this lady up if nothing else – but that didn't feel right to me at all and so I stuck to my guns.

At the end of the circle I took the man to one side and gave him the message one-to-one. As I'd expected, he got quite emotional but after we'd finished he thanked me for respecting his privacy rather than giving the message in front of everyone.

And that's not the only time I've done it; in fact, I'm probably a bit of a pain in the bum for the presidents of churches near me! I'm more than happy to go along and do my thing, give messages and learn from other mediums. But the minute something doesn't feel right, I'm out.

If you don't feel comfortable working with Spirit in a particular place or environment then, no matter what anyone else says, you don't have to. Because of that though, make sure you test a place or an environment out before you commit to doing something for someone. If you promise to be the medium on a paranormal investigation night to a particularly haunted location then you really need to make sure that you're comfortable and confident in that location before you agree to it, because if you're anything like me then letting someone down who you've promised to help out is almost as scary an idea as working somewhere that feels really terrifying or unpleasant.

And a similar idea applies to the ways in which you work with Spirit too. Since I stopped telling people I was training to be a medium (which I did for a long time) and started referring to myself as an actual medium a few years ago, I've had countless people ask me for a private sittings, where they would pay me to sit with them one-on-one for half an hour or more and pass on messages to them from Spirit. It's not something I'm against doing and is something I'll do quite comfortably when the time is right. But recently I've quite a lot on my plate and honestly don't know how I could fit in one or more extra hour of work each week. However, I did want to use my mediumship to help as many people as I could. So, rather than give private sittings, I started offering channelled letters (more on those in Chapter 14) which I email or post out to people when they're done. I love doing the letters, but the biggest benefit of working that way is that I can do it on the sofa in my pyjamas if I want to, and no one need ever know about it...except maybe you!

Mediumship is like anything, just because other people do it a certain way doesn't necessarily mean you should do it the same way. In fact there are times when doing it a different way is actually better for you because it makes you more unique! That's not to say you can't learn from the way others do things though. Whatever it is that you do with your time and energy, I'm very much of the opinion that the best way to learn how to do something is to look at what other people do, take the bits you like and that feel right and then throw everything else away.

Working when it feels right

We've touched on it a bit elsewhere but one thing that can't be underestimated is the need to only work with Spirit when it feels right and comfortable for you to do that.

If you're feeling tired, stressed, unwell, or even really

unhappy, then maybe you're not in the right frame of mind to work with Spirit. Some people will tell you that working with Spirit will always make you feel better so you should do it even when you're not feeling your best, and it's true that sometimes the Spirit world can generate so much positive energy that everything seems better. But there are some times when you just can't or don't have the energy to give out in the first place.

In those cases remember that looking after yourself is the most important thing; aside from talk about protection and intentions, if you try to do anything when you're not feeling up to it, then the chances are that you won't do the best job you could, and that's not fair on the people and Spirits that you're working with or on yourself.

Remember to go easy on yourself – you may be a medium but that doesn't mean that life is any easier or that the difficult things become any less painful. In fact sometimes, they're even harder to deal with. So if something happens – particularly something like the death of someone close – that leads you to think you need to take a bit of a break from working with Spirit, whether that be one day or a few weeks, then do that. Keeping yourself safe will only ever make you a better medium.

Working with other people

The majority of people who come to mediums will be genuine people who come looking for guidance, help or proof of life after death. If you're able to give them what they're looking for, most will walk away smiling; and even if you're not, most will understand that you did your best and that maybe it's just not the right time for them to hear the information that they're searching for.

Unfortunately, you will sometimes come across people who want to hear from Spirit for less-than-positive reasons or people who are so desperate for whatever they're looking for that they will become angry, clingy or all-out nasty with anyone who can't give them that information. And sometimes you will come across people who are so sceptical about the idea of life after death, or so completely against the idea of communicating with Spirit, that they will be mean, dismissive or aggressive no matter how hard you work and how much amazing proof you give them.

I'm pleased to say that these people are generally pretty few and far between, but you will probably come across at least a handful of them in the time that you work with Spirit. Learning to spot and to deal with those people will come with practice, but nine times out of ten you will just *know* who is going to be a challenge to work with by the way you feel about them. If you find yourself having to deal with someone like that remember to continue listening to your gut – if it told you to watch out for them in the first place it will, more than likely, be able to help you out with how to deal with them too.

Trust

As I said at the very start of this chapter, the most important person to listen to when it comes to working with Spirit is you. And I don't mean that little voice in your head which tells you you're rubbish and that talking to dead people is far too special or scary for someone like you to do... I mean the true part of yourself that sits in your heart, your stomach or wherever else feels right for you.

It's not always possible to follow your gut in all areas of your life ("My gut says don't go to school or work this morning even though I have an important exam or meeting. OK then, I'd best stay in bed!"), but working with Spirit is the one area where it's not just possible, it is really important. And although that may seem difficult, and maybe even a little crazy at first, it won't take long at all before you realise just how important it is to listen to and follow your gut.

It's always important to trust your instincts, even when they seem wrong or silly. I've lost count of the number of times my gut has screamed something particular at me, only for me to ignore it completely and find out later that actually it had been right all along.

I'd like to think that one day I'll learn but no matter how much I may or may not work with Spirit, I'm still only human this time around, and being human means that means that we will all make mistakes! But as long as we go easy on ourselves when that happens, and remember to learn from them, we won't go far wrong.

Chapter Thirteen

Bringing Spirit into your everyday life

It's lovely to be able to help other people and to bring them the comfort, healing and guidance they're looking for from Spirit. But it can be frustrating to give amazing messages that really make a difference to other people and not be able to get the same sort of information for yourself.

Mediums can't always demand particular information from Spirit, get in touch with specific people from the Other Side or use their connection to gain an easy ride through life, but there are things that all of us – especially those who are already open to the Spirit world – can do to bring the wisdom, knowledge and love of Spirit into our everyday lives.

For starters, we mediums have two things a lot easier than others do, in that we know death is nothing to be afraid of when the time comes and we know there is always someone looking out for us no matter where we are or what we do. They might not sound it, but those things cause some people an awful lot of unhappiness, so to know for certain that they're nothing to worry about is quite a blessing in itself.

Asking for help and guidance

The other thing we know is that our Guides, loved ones and other helpers are always there to give help or guidance whenever we need it. The Spirit world may not always give us the clear and detailed guidance we're hoping for, and it can be difficult to tell the difference between what they are saying and what we want to hear, but we do know that they will speak to us if we quieten our minds enough to listen.

If you're struggling to ask for help and guidance for yourself then the short exercise below might be a good way to try it out.

1. Sit quietly in a place where you won't be disturbed, close your eyes and breathe deeply as you call in your protection;

2. Open up your energies and call our to your Guides, helpers, Angels, Inspirers and loved ones; invite them all to step forward and work with you now;

3. Explain to your helpers, either out loud or in your head, what it is that you're struggling with and where you feel that you need their guidance;

4. Sit quietly for a while and see what comes to mind, focus on the things that come to you from Spirit rather than those you recognise as your own thoughts and ideas;

5. If you feel you need it, ask your Guides and helpers to show you a sign over the coming days to confirm that you are understanding their guidance properly;

6. Thank your helpers for their time and guidance and ask them to be with you and help you over the coming days as you take your next steps in this situation;

7. Work to close your energies back down again, continue to breathe deeply. When you're ready, open your eyes and come back into the room.

Remember that the guidance you get from Spirit won't necessarily tell you exactly what to do, or what is going to happen. That's not because the Spirit world doesn't care, it's because you have to make your own choices in order to grow and learn and become stronger and wiser. Spirits will always do their best to guide you along the right path for you though and will give you any help you need in that way.

Sometimes we ask the Spirit world for guidance only to realise later that maybe what they'd told us was wrong; or that's what I've thought in the past. A few years ago I was in a difficult relationship and asked Spirit regularly for help and guidance. Everything I was told seemed to suggest that I should stick with the relationship and everything would be fine. Well, lo and behold that wasn't the case at all – actually the situation just got worse until I ended up heartbroken and unhappy.

At the time I couldn't understand how Spirit had gotten things so wrong...but then I looked back over the messages, readings and signs and realised that Spirit had never said the relationship would work out fine, I'd just interpreted it that way because it was what I wanted to hear. But everything Spirit had told me was right and has been proved that way many times since.

Of course life might have been easier if I'd listened to what Spirit was trying to tell me back then, rather than hearing the messages the way I wanted to, but I learned some important lessons from that relationship, and came out of it much stronger than I had been.

So when asking for guidance for yourself remember to try and listen to what is actually being said and what feels right rather than what you want to hear.

Signs

We've already talked about the signs Spirits send to back up something they've told us or to point us in the right direction. As a medium you may recognise and understand those signs better than many people because you are already open to the idea of Spirit communicating with you.

If you want to check out your understanding of any information you've received from Spirit, or if you're looking for some guidance on what to do next then you can always ask your Guides and helpers for a sign.

Again, sit quietly, call out to your Guides and helpers and ask them to give you a sign of which way to turn, or that you've understood their message correctly. Give them an idea of the sign you would like to see, and ask them to help you not only spot the sign but recognise it as being the sign that you've asked for.

When it comes to the sign you would like you can ask for anything, from traditional things like feathers, butterflies and shooting stars to whatever else floats your boat; I've asked for all sorts over the years, from actual words and messages to particular plants or colours or models of cars. Or you can just leave it up to the universe and ask them to send whichever sign is right for you and to help you to recognise it.

Whatever you ask for, the trick is then to sit back and wait for it. Keep your eyes open but don't spend too much energy looking for your sign because as the old saying goes – a watched pot never boils! Just have faith that if you're right your Guides will send you a sign.

A friend of mine was looking for a new house and went to visit countless houses. The only one that felt right was the first one she viewed but it was smaller than she wanted and not quite in the right area. Eventually she asked Spirit to show her the right house by sending a rainbow. After more house viewings she finally went back to the very first one, thinking that the smaller bedrooms were a small price to pay for such a lovely little house. As she got out of the car there, over the top of the house, was a great big rainbow! My friend and her family are now very happy in their cosy, beautiful new house.

One of the best things about being open to Spirit is that we find it easier to recognise those extra signs we don't ask for which come to show us that Spirit is with us or that we're on the right path. Things like the shower of white feathers that suddenly appeared in my garden one morning (with no poorly bird to be found I'm pleased to say) or the very symbolic dreams that seem to tell us exactly where to go next.

Being open to Spirit means that we know we not only recognise those signs but can appreciate them for what they are rather than pass them off as a coincidence or fluke.

Protection

In case you hadn't already noticed, I think protection is kind of important when it comes to working with Spirit (I know, I've barely mentioned it...). But protecting yourself regularly can help you even more than just in your work with Spirit.

A few months ago I took my dog out for a walk. It was a little later than we'd usually go and I wasn't completely comfortable on my own so as we set off I asked Archangel Michael to surround us both with his blue light of protection and to keep us company on our walk.

When we reached the park there was a group of drunk guys there causing trouble; shouting, swearing and throwing bottles which were shattering on the path. Unfortunately, I only spotted them when they started making noise, by which point they were in the middle of the path right in front of us and we had no way of avoiding them other than just walking right next to them.

I'm not the biggest and scariest of people, and although Kali can look scary to some people she's actually pretty small and is quite timid around people who are making a lot of noise, so we both flinched when the bottles started flying. Again I quietly spoke to Archangel Michael and asked for his protection...and sure enough we walked right in between the two main trouble-makers – close enough to touch them, but they didn't even bat an eyelid at us, it was like we were invisible!

That isn't to say that Spirit will protect you from anything negative, painful or scary because, again, not all of the lessons we have to learn are nice ones. But the protection techniques we use to work with Spirit can play a big part in keeping us as safe as possible in our daily lives too and can always be called on for help when we encounter anything negative or scary.

Of course those techniques aren't just useful for looking after ourselves, they can also help protect those we love too. And the more you work on and build confidence in your own protection, the more you will trust it to take care of the people and things that are important to you.

The bigger picture

One of the best, and also worst, things for me about working so closely with the Spirit world is that it helps me to see the bigger picture a lot better. The messages I've given and received over the years have all helped me to understand that everything that happens to any of us is part of a much bigger picture of helping ourselves and each other to learn and grow.

Although I can't say it makes me perfect (I'm still only human after all!), being able to see that bigger picture does tend to make it easier for me to rise above the little things. Don't get me wrong, things still irritate me sometimes, but it's generally much easier nowadays not to worry about what someone has said or done and instead focus on what I can learn from that person or situation.

That's not to say that some things don't still hurt though. I get as upset as anyone when someone I care about is hurt or worse, even if I can see what they and everyone around them is learning from that situation. However, it can make it that little easier to be able to talk things over with Spirit, and see the bigger picture in the situation.

Next time you find yourself in a difficult situation, try to think about what you're learning from this situation and about the lessons you want to teach through this too.

Connecting through other mediums

No matter how long you work with Spirit it's always nice to get a message from Spirit through someone else who doesn't know what's going on in your head. And the more time you spend around other mediums, the more you will learn the ones whose messages you can trust completely.

But the more you work with Spirit and the stronger your connection grows, it's likely that you'll look for that validation from someone else less and less. Maybe because you trust your own connection more, or maybe because you just have more faith that things will work out as they're supposed to and that everything will be OK. Either way though, it's always nice to know that there are words of wisdom and comfort on hand from Spirit as and when you need them.

Getting in touch with your own Spirit

The best and easiest way to embrace all of the loveliness of Spirit is to get in touch with the most important Spirit of all – your own inner self.

Each of us is a beautiful and perfect Spirit but over time we allow situations and people to convince us of who and what we should be; and let ourselves get caught up in fear and worry which distracts us from being as happy and as calm as we could be.

The easiest way to get in touch with your own inner or spiritual self is to listen to your gut and to your heart and then act upon what those things are telling you. Life can be busy at times and we all have things that we don't like doing, but even spending just a few minutes every day doing something which refreshes you and makes you feel truly happy can make those things seem so much easier. For me it's singing – even if it's just in the car or the shower – and walking my dog; simple things, but doing them helps me to feel instantly better and makes me feel alive again after a bad day.

We've talked already about how important it is to listen to your intuition, and the more you do that, the more you'll learn to trust it. And the more you trust that little voice inside you, the easier you will find it to get in touch with and follow that guidance. I can't promise what your intuition suggests will always be easy but following that inner wisdom and knowing will help you to find the way that's best for you, and to become a stronger and happier person in the long run.

Chapter Fourteen

Different ways of working

So far in this book we've talked a lot about traditional mediumship where you sit down with someone one-to-one or stand in front of a group of people and talk through the messages that Spirit gives those people.

But there are many different ways to work with the Spirit world, some of which work better for some people than others and some of which can be really interesting to try.

This chapter includes details of a few of the different types of mediumship, along with some suggested exercises if you would like to try them out. Give the ones that interest you a go, or give them all a go if you would like to, and see which ones come easiest or seem most interesting. Remember though, whatever tools or spiritual skills you use, invoke your protection as always and make sure you're doing this for all of the right reasons.

Cards

One very popular tool for connecting with Spirit is cards; usually you will find people using either tarot cards or oracle cards such as Angel cards.

All tarot cards follow the same basic format of fifteen Major Arcana cards (such as the High Priestess, the Emperor and the Sun) as well as a further fifty-six Minor Arcana cards which are split into four suits (usually cups, pentacles, wands and swords – although different decks of cards may call these different things) numbered from ace to ten, with a page, knight, king and queen for each suit too. Although the meanings of each card may differ slightly between different decks, each card within the tarot has a specific meaning which can be built upon or influenced by the other cards next to it in a spread.

Oracle cards are a bit different to tarot. They are decks of cards, usually all following the same theme such as Angels or animals, each of which has its own meaning. Oracle cards can be quite simple to learn because each card has a title and meaning written on it, but of course it's all down to personal preference.

One of my favourite things about cards is that they can make it easier to pick up guidance for yourself without worrying about your brain or heart getting in the way.

And when you're trying to pick up messages for other people, even just a very quick reading can often be a good way to help tune into the person you're working with and their helpers and loved ones on the Other Side.

The best and only way to try working with cards for yourself is to get your hands on a pack and give it a go; you can buy tarot and oracle cards on Amazon and in most good bookshops or alternative shops, but they often cost over £10 a pack.

When you're trying to decide on a deck of cards (because there are plenty out there!), go for the set that feels right; hold each pack in your hands and see how you feel about them before committing to buy anything. But don't stress – remember that the right cards will come to you at exactly the right time, even if that means waiting longer than you wanted to!

If you can't get your hands on a deck of tarot or oracle cards then you may wish to practice with a deck of normal playing cards instead. Our traditional playing cards are said to be based on the Minor Arcana of the tarot deck, so can work just as well for connecting with Spirit. I don't know a great deal about reading playing cards but there are books and websites out there which can get you started with that.

Whatever you use, take time to get to know your cards before you read them; hold them in your hands and allow your energies to link with them then focus on each card in turn and think about what it means and feels like to you. Of course, the traditional meanings and those you read in the guidebook that comes with the cards will be important, but your thoughts and feelings about your cards are just as important when you're reading with them.

Scrying

We've probably all seen pictures or movies of psychics predicting the future by looking into a crystal ball or scrying. Scrying means using a reflective surface to pick up images and information from Spirit and although you can use water, a mirror or any other reflective surface to do that, crystals carry such powerful energies that they're the best things to start with if you can.

Many people like crystals without really understanding just how powerful these beautiful stones are. We've already talked about using crystals for protection, to help raise your vibrations or to ground yourself. But communicating with and picking information up from Spirit is just another way that they can be used.

When you first start to scry, the images you see may be quite vague and you could be forgiven for thinking that you're just imagining them, or that they're just made up of shapes that were already in the crystal to start with. But as with any type of Spirit communication the more you practice, the clearer and more detailed those images will become, and the more information you will be able to pick up.

You can use good old-fashioned crystal balls for scrying, but any reasonably clear crystal with an even surface big enough to look into will do the job. Some of the best crystals to use for scrying are amethyst, rose quartz, clear quartz and smoky quartz, so if you can find a piece with at least one smooth side you can look into, then you're ready to go.

If you're scrying for the first time, go through your usual protection and opening up and then look into whatever it is you're using to scry. Try to clear your mind by focusing on the crystal and try not to look too hard for images in the surface; I know that's easier said than done so if it helps then try and focus on any cracks, blemishes or shapes that you can see already within the crystal and then see what else you start to see within those shapes, behind them or out of the corner of your eye.

Dowsing

Another use for crystals is dowsing, which is generally a very straightforward way to communicate with Spirit as it involves asking for yes or no answers to the questions you ask.

Dowsing isn't just something that only spiritually aware people use, it has been used by very down-to-earth people for centuries as a way to find water, ley lines or (more recently) electricity. When my friend's mum first met her dad, a farmer, she was amazed when he started dowsing for water. My friend's mum asked whether he was asking for spiritual guidance and he just laughed – of course not, dowsing is just something that farmers do!

There are two main ways to dowse, using either pendulums or rods, but both work in similar ways, by moving one way if the answer is yes and another for no.

Dowsing rods are twigs or bits of metal shaped like the letter L, with a small handle and a longer piece that points out in front. As you hold them and ask questions, you will feel the sticks twist in a particular way depending on the answer to your question. The ways they move for each are different for everyone, so it's up to you to learn which way is which.

The other way to dowse with rods is to use them to search for something. In that case you would walk around somewhere with the sticks in front of you, or hold them over a map, and wait for the rods to cross over wherever the item is.

Dowsing with pendulums is similar but works in a different way: a pendulum can be any weighted object that hangs from a string or chain. The most popular pendulums are often crystals but you can use anything. Many older ladies talk about hanging their wedding rings from a string to use as pendulums and I've found that the best and most reliable pendulum I have is the necklace I wear every day.

You will probably already have heard of people dowsing with pendulums because again, it's something that has been done for many many years. The most common example is those people who hang a pendulum over a pregnant lady's bump to find out what sex her baby is. And although we usually ask our pendulums for a yes or a no answer, that just goes to show that dowsing can be used to answer any question where there are two possible answers.

In the same way that rods will move in a particular direction to answer your question, pendulums will swing in a particular way depending on the answer; some may swing in either clockwise or anti-clockwise circles or move from side to side or backwards and forwards.

The main thing to watch out for with dowsing though is manipulating the results that you get from your rods or pendulum. Often that's not something you mean to do, but a shaky hand can make it very easy for a pendulum to change direction or motion, even if you don't realise you're doing it. With rods, having them slightly weighted or bent in the wrong way can affect the way they turn or move, so be wary of that too. Ways to get around this are to look for a heavier pendulum which is harder to move by accident and to use either ready-made balanced rods or simple home-made rods which leave less room for differences in weights.

One of the simplest ways to make dowsing rods is to get two pieces of coat-hanger wire of the same length and bend them into L shapes. Remember though that wire can be sharp and difficult to cut and bend so it's a good idea to get help from someone stronger who has the proper tools to hand.

To practice dowsing, either find or make a set of rods or a pendulum (or if you have both handy then try each one and see what works best for you) and sit quietly with them. Do your usual opening-up and protection routine and then ask, either out loud or in your head that if there is anyone there prepared to work with you they show you a yes answer. You may need to do this a couple of times, or to keep asking the same question, but you should find that the pendulum or rods start to move in a particular direction. Take note of what that direction is and then either set the rods back to centre or stop the pendulum moving and hold it still. Then do the same thing again but asking for a no answer instead.

Once you have your yes and no answers you can ask pretty much any questions you like, but remember that asking questions about the future doesn't necessarily give definite answers as the future can always be changed.

Automatic writing

Automatic writing is one of my favourite ways to work with Spirit. That's partly because, as I've said before, automatic writing is something I can do on the sofa in my pyjamas if I want to, but also because as someone who loves to read and write, writing on behalf of Spirit always makes me smile!

Automatic writing is when you open yourself up to the Spirit world then sit down with a pen and paper, or with a computer, and allow it to write through you. It can be quite scary at first to watch your fingers moving without really knowing what they're going to say, or to suddenly look up from the TV and realise that you've been typing for the last half hour without thinking, but as long as you're careful with your protection then there's no need to be afraid.

I was fascinated by automatic writing from the first time I heard about it, and I regularly used to sit down with a pen and paper like I'd been told, and will Spirit to write through me. I tried for years and ended up with nothing but a few random words and a bit of a scrawl. Then one day I decided to try a more modern way; I sat down in front of the computer, opened up and...wow, there was no stopping the messages!

But what use is automatic writing? Personally, I use it to write messages for people, although I've heard speeches and meditations and have read blogs, poems and even books that have apparently been channelled from Spirit. So the only real way to figure out the best use for your own automatic writing is to give it a go and see what comes through.

And yes, I have tried automatic writing when it comes to assignments for college and reports from work; sometimes it works, but usually Spirit much prefers to let me get on with the hard work on my own.

When I first started trying to work with the Spirit world in this way I used to wonder how I would know that what I was writing had come from them. Sometimes it can be as easy as the fact that you almost switch off and don't even realise you are typing or writing until suddenly you look up and there are hundreds of words on the page; at other times you can write for ages then read your words back only to realise you don't remember any of what you'd just written.

So how do you practice automatic writing? Just open up in the way you usually would then sit down with either a pen and paper or a computer, and ask Sprit to communicate with you in writing.

One of the best figures to call upon when you're opening up to do this is Archangel Gabriel, the communicator Angel. You can ask him to help you establish a clear channel of communication with Spirit and to produce the most perfect piece of spiritual writing possible, and then allow him to do his thing.

Don't be put off if it takes you a while to get anything that makes any sense or if the first few times you do this you get nothing at all. But try to relax and almost distract your mind then allow things to flow as and when they're supposed to.

Psychic art

Just like with automatic writing it is possible to allow Spirit to draw through you. Often psychic artists will draw the people they see or will draw scenes that Spirit is showing to them, either from the past or from the Spirit world.

I'm rubbish at drawing and maybe because of that lack of confidence, I've so far never been able to master psychic art either but I do know a very good psychic artist and his drawings, which seem to come from nowhere, always amaze me.

As with automatic writing it's easy to wonder what you would ever use psychic art for, but a lot of people like to have drawings of their Guides or of their lost loved ones. The more scenic images can bring back lovely memories for people, help them feel better about a situation, or even be used for healing or meditation.

Practicing psychic art is similar to automatic writing, but rather than a pen or keyboard you sit down with a pencil, paints or some other art equipment and invite the Spirit world to use you as their artist. Again, it can take a while to get anything particularly clear or detailed but keep going and over time you will find that your pictures become clearer and clearer and you are able to include more detail in them.

Psychometry

Some mediums ask for photographs, jewellery or other personal items while they connect with and pass on messages from Spirit, and this is psychometry.

By holding an object that belongs or links to someone, some people can connect with the energy of that person, making it easier to pick up messages from Spirit which not only link to the object itself but to the person who has given it to you.

Psychometry can also involve touching the person you are trying to pass messages on to, although I would recommend being careful with that. Holding someone's hand or touching their arm while passing on a message may make it easier to connect with their energies and the Spirits who are trying to communicate with them, but it could also leave you a little too close for comfort, either physically or in terms of the strong energies and emotions you pick up both from Spirit and the physical person. And if you choose to touch someone at the start of a session it can make it awkward to move away later if it starts to feel uncomfortable or unnecessary.

Some people think psychometry is an easy or fake type of mediumship, because there may already be a lot that you can tell about someone from a personal object. However, providing the information you're giving is more detailed than the obvious then that can be a very unfair criticism.

Psychometry can be a great way to start working and communicating with a person's Spirit helpers and although there's no definite way of demanding to speak to particular Spirits or to force the Spirit world to talk about a particular subject, psychometry can be a good way to try and focus your mind on a particular person or topic.

It's difficult to try psychometry on your own so you will need the help of a friend for this one...ask someone you trust and are comfortable with (and who is also comfortable trying this with you) to bring along a photo or personal object, ideally one that you know nothing about, and sit with you for a while.

Protect yourself and open up as usual and then ask Spirit to attune you to the object and any messages they have for that person. Then wait and see what images, words, phrases or impressions come through to you as you hold the object.

Remember that even the smallest message can mean a lot to some people, so give the person in front of you as much information as you can and ask for their feedback.

Healing

For many people working with Spirit isn't necessarily about passing on messages, it is about passing on positive energy to help heal someone in some way. There are lots of different types of spiritual healing, many of which involve specific training, but the basic idea behind all of them is the same – we put our hands on someone or something that needs healing and ask for Spirit to send that energy through us.

I've personally experienced spiritual healing help with all sorts of problems – physical, emotional and mental in people, animals, plants and situations. But no matter how effective you become at spiritual healing, it's important to remember that you are not a doctor. And it's also important never to promise to be able to heal or cure anything.

If spiritual healing is something you're very interested in you can look into things like Reiki, crystal healing and other energy-related healing methods. However, I believe you can give basic spiritual healing a go without any training as long as you protect yourself and the person you're working with, get their permission and set the intentions to provide the most perfect form of healing possible.

If you don't have another person to work with then try some spiritual healing on yourself the next time you have a headache, stomach upset or any other to fix the problem. Open up and protect yourself as usual then place your hands on the affected area (as long as it's OK to do so) and ask Spirit to help you provide the most perfect healing possible.

You may also want to call on Archangel Raphael, the doctor of the Angels, or to call on your own specialist healing Guide to help you with this. Then sit back and concentrate on how this feels.

Often you will be able to feel positive energy flowing out of your hands and into the person, although every spiritual healer feels this energy differently. Pay attention to what you pick up while you are giving healing too, you may find out you come across other messages or information from Spirit.

Whenever you conduct spiritual healing remember to cleanse

yourself afterwards to prevent carrying away any of the negativity or harmful energy that needed to be healed in the first place. The easiest way to do this is to wash your hands in cold water and then protect yourself all over again, although there are plenty of other ways to cleanse your energies if that doesn't feel right for you.

Animal communication

Remember that every living thing has a Spirit, so communicating with Spirit doesn't necessarily just mean communicating with those who are already in the Spirit world. It can also be used to communicate with those souls here are on Earth who can't talk to us in the usual ways, such as our animal friends.

Think about how many times you've looked at your pets and thought you knew what they were thinking. By working with yours and your animal's Guides to connect with your pet's soul or higher self more clearly, you may be able to pick up more about what they are trying to tell you.

The easiest way to do this is to protect yourself and your pet and open up as usual, before either putting your hand on your pet or looking into their eyes and asking your Guides to speak with their Guides and help you communicate more clearly with one another.

Whenever you are working with animals remember to keep yourself safe and to keep the animal safe too. Some animals aren't comfortable with you working so deeply with them so it's important to back off and leave them be anytime your pet starts getting agitated or uncomfortable. Be especially careful if you work with any animals other than your own pets that you don't necessarily know particularly well, or who don't know you.

Whichever type of mediumship you try, remember to protect yourself beforehand as always and to ground yourself once you're finished. After all, remember that keeping yourself safe is the most important part of working with Spirit.

It's also important to remember to give yourself time with any new type of mediumship you decide to try; if one of the suggestions above really interests you but you don't get very far on your first attempt, don't just give up. These things can take time but the more you practice and relax, the easier it will be to improve, and the stronger your abilities will become in the long run.

It's often worth writing down what you get when you first start trying something new. It may mean nothing at first but over time you might just come to find that your first few attempts at something were actually pretty good!

Below are two more tools or types of work with the Spirit world that you are likely to hear about, and that some people may be drawn to try. However, I can't stress enough that each of the following ways of working can be dangerous if they're not done properly. For that reason I would strongly advise you not to try any of the following until you are completely confident in your own protection and Guides, are somewhere safe and, wherever possible, are in the company of an experienced medium who you trust.

Channelling or trance mediumship

We've already talked about acting as a channel for Spirit through automatic writing or psychic art, but the purest form of 'channelling' Spirit is trance mediumship, where a medium literally steps aside and allows Spirit to talk through them.

Watching someone in trance is quite strange, as you can see them sitting in front of you but the words – and often the voice – coming out of their mouth isn't at all theirs. And being the medium in a trance is even stranger; you can feel your body and can hear yourself speaking but have very little control over what is being said or done, and can almost hear someone else in your head with you.

The weirdest thing I've ever experienced is when a Spirit not only takes over a medium's voice but their face and changes the medium's face to look like their own, something called physical mediumship.

If you're watching this happen you can literally see the medium's face and other physical features such as their hair and even glasses, change to look like another person; and in my experience if you're the medium whose face is being taken over it's even stranger. For me it always feels like my face is full of pins and needles – although not in an unpleasant way – and being moved about in strange ways. I've never seen my own face change, because the idea freaks me out, but I've been told what it's like and have also seen it happen to other mediums, and it's both amazing and very weird!

As you can imagine, this can be very dangerous because stepping your own Spirit aside and allowing someone else to take over your mouth, voice or face means giving up control of your own body and relying completely on your Guides to keep you safe. Not only that though, if a particularly pushy, strong or selfish Spirit is allowed to step forward and work through you, you could find yourself with a fight on your hands to get back to yourself which can be very scary not to mention tiring emotionally, physically, spiritually and mentally.

Ouija boards

One spiritual tool that used to be very popular is Ouija or letter boards, and if you're a fan of scary films or ghost stories you'll probably have heard of these boards which invite Spirits to come forward and give or spell out answers to the questions they're asked by moving a glass which is being gently touched by everyone around the board.

In theory, these sound like a great and very simple way to communicate with Spirit, but most people who used them to communicate with the Other Side did so without protecting themselves or asking for the right sort of help.

That meant that any old Spirits were able to step forward and communicate, opening the door up for negative or dangerous energies to come forward and not only talk through the board but sneak in to attach themselves more closely to the people who called them up in the first place, scaring them, draining their energies and doing goodness knows what else.

The other problem with these boards was the potential for someone around the circle to play games...to make a Ouija board work, everyone around the board is supposed to put one finger on the glass in the centre. But of course it's very easy for one or more people to do more than just gently touch the glass and instead push it around to spell out whatever it is that they want the board to say.

Just like tarot cards, dowsing rods and pendulums, Ouija boards themselves aren't necessarily negative things. However, they can be dangerous if they are not used with the proper precautions or in the right environment. I would recommend only using a Ouija board as part of a genuine experiment with a group of people who have protected themselves properly, are carrying the right intention and, ideally, have an experienced medium with them.

If you're asked to use a Ouija board (or any other spiritual tool for that matter) for fun, without any protection or with a load of people who don't know what they're doing then I only have one piece of advice – don't!

Chapter Fifteen

Next steps

This book has tried to cover everything you might need to know when you're starting your journey as a medium, based on the lessons I've learned and the mistakes I've made too!

Combine this information with guidance from your own spiritual helpers and from your inner self, and remember the key elements of protection and intention, and I'm certain that you'll never go far wrong in your work with Spirit.

However, a book will only ever provide you with a starting point on your journey with Spirit. So, now that's finished, where do you go next?

Unfortunately, as I write this, there still aren't too many places or organisations out there specifically for young mediums. But that makes it even more important to get help and support from a place that's right for you.

Spiritualist churches

It's completely your choice but your local spiritualist church is likely to be a good starting point. Firstly they're free (but more on that in a minute) and secondly they should always be operating with the best possible intentions.

As a starter you'll find a list of local spiritualist churches on the website for your country's union, federation or association of spiritualism. Obviously you want to find the church that's nearest to you and is easiest to get to, but it's also important to make sure that the church you're going to is somewhere that you feel comfortable and safe.

If there are a few churches around you, it can make sense to try a few out and find the church you're most comfortable with. If you're already working with your intuition you will know which is the best church for you just by listening to your own inner guidance and paying attention to the way you feel in a particular place.

It's worth remembering that some spiritualist churches can be a bit funny about under-eighteens going into their services or events alone. If you're under eighteen and are unsure about this, you could call or email the church first to check that out, or take someone older along with you on your first trip for moral support if nothing else.

It can be quite daunting to go to a spiritualist church for the first time, and quite confusing to know which of their services to go along to. If you're looking for a more religious service with one medium standing at the front of the room giving messages out, their Sunday service is the place to be.

However, if you want to develop and test out your own connection with Spirit, you might be better off going along to their open circle. These services still include prayers, and sometimes a bit of singing too, but they are much less religious in that they tend to be more about mediums of all levels of experience getting together and then standing up to give whatever messages they have for the other people in the room.

Development circles

Another great place to work on your development is in a home or development circle. These are smaller development groups that tend to meet at the home of an experienced medium so that everyone in the group can work on their own development somewhere safe and helpful.

The only downside of development circles like this is that you generally have to be invited to them, and that is often a case of knowing the right people at the right time.

If you are invited to a development circle where you would feel safe and with someone that you trust then by all means go along. If you go along and it feels right, great – enjoy and take from it everything that you can. But if it doesn't feel right, or if at any point you find yourself feeling unsafe or uncomfortable, then maybe it's time to leave that circle and move on to a different development group or tactic.

Other development classes

There are plenty of other classes, workshops and groups to think about if you're serious about training as a medium. But there are a few really important things to consider when you're looking for the right place to develop.

- Money: Some classes and workshops out there cost an awful lot of money although some equally good classes cost little or nothing to go along to. I would argue that genuine spiritual teachers will keep their costs as low as possible so that the people who really need and want to develop can do so. If something is going to cost you a small fortune, I would suggest at least looking around and giving a free or cheaper class a go first before you commit to anything else.

- The teacher: A teacher is one of the most important parts of any development class. Firstly, are they a good medium themselves? Mediumship is really one of those things that you need to know how to do yourself, and how to keep the people you're working with safe, before you teach it, so make sure you know a bit about your teacher's reputation and abilities before you join their group. Make sure that you feel safe and comfortable around your teacher too – learning to be a medium can be scary and emotional at times so it's important that your teacher is someone you can go to if you're upset, scared or unsure, and who you know will have your back whatever happens in or out of your classes.

- Safety: This is far and away the most important thing to

concentrate on when you're working with Spirit so, wherever you choose to go to, make sure that you're safe, not just spiritually and emotionally but physically too. Make sure someone always knows where you're going and that there is someone else in the group who you know you can trust. If the group is held on an evening, make arrangements to get to and from the class every week safely so you never have to worry about getting home while you're there, as it will only pre-occupy your mind while you're trying to work.

- Patience: It's easy to be impatient at first but try not to stress or worry too much if you can't immediately find somewhere to develop. If that happens, ask your Guides and helpers for support and guidance in finding the right environment in which you can develop and then just try your best to be patient. Remember that the right development will come along for you at the right time. And if that takes a while don't worry, there are plenty of exercises in this book and elsewhere that you can do safely on your own to keep developing until the right class or group comes along.

Wherever you choose to go to develop, try the environment out first and see how it feels. Remember that your Guides and intuition will know best when it comes to what and where is right for you so listen to that guidance, and if you're not happy then look elsewhere!

Like me, you may decide to work on your development alone rather than go through a formal development process. I can't exactly criticise you for making that decision but it's important to remember that I was lucky – I come from a spiritually open family who've always been there to help, support and advise me, and have a best friend who was going through her own development journey at the same time.

Unless you have one or more people in your life with the same interests or experiences who will be able to at least support you, I would strongly advise you not to try developing alone. As we've said, working with Spirit can be scary and difficult so it's really important to have support through that and to have someone on hand in case anything does go wrong or gets a little bit too much.

However you choose to develop, it's important to remember that this is your journey and is something you must do at your own pace. Don't let anyone try to rush you to do or try anything that you're not comfortable with or don't feel ready for, but also don't let anyone hold you back if you truly genuinely feel that you're ready for the next step.

One spiritualist church went through a phase of trying to force me to take Sunday services. It's not something I would be uncomfortable doing, but at the time things were very busy for me and my Sundays were incredibly precious free time...yet no one at the church seemed to understand that. On the other side of that, a while ago I realised that none of the development classes I'd come across offered exactly what I was looking for and decided to start my own home circle. A lot of people told me I couldn't and shouldn't do that because I was too young and for a while I listened to them. But eventually I decided to follow my gut and wow I'm glad I did...our little home circle is an amazing environment that goes from strength to strength every time we meet and it's something we're all really proud of.

Once you start any sort of formal spiritual development programme it's important to stay committed. A lot of people will tell you that opening up to Spirit is easier if you do it in the same place and at the same time each week or month; I don't fully agree with that but I do think that if you want to develop the bond with your Spirit helpers and your connection with the Spirit world then it is important to put the effort in and to give the same amount of respect to your Spirit friends as you would to those in the physical world.

For that reason, make sure that any class or group you sign up to is one that you can get to regularly. Holidays, sickness and other random things will always stop you getting to every single meeting, but it's important to make it to the majority of sessions for the sake of your own development and for the other members of your group.

Being a medium is amazing, not just because of the good you can do for other people but because of what you gain from it and from the whole experience of working with Spirit too. Not only does it build your connection with the Spirit world but it also helps with more day-to-day things too, such as trust in yourself and your own abilities and the confidence to stand up and talk to people you might not have otherwise spoken to.

The absolute best thing about being a medium though, for me, is just the fact that it's pretty blooming cool. You get to see, hear and learn about some really interesting things and to play your part in helping people to heal, grow and develop.

For a long time now mediumship has been done in the same way and although some bits of that old school are great, others could do with a bit of updating. People like you will form the next generation of mediums so it's down to you to make the future of mediumship a bright, exciting and positive one, and I wish you all of the very best of luck and support with that.

Whatever you choose to do and wherever your spiritual journey takes you, remember the two most important rules – protect yourself, and hold the right intention to guarantee the best and most positive results possible.

Soul Rocks is a fresh list that takes the search for soul and spirit mainstream. Chick-lit, young adult, cult, fashionable fiction & non-fiction with a fierce twist